THE ADMINISTRATIVE PROCESS

STORRS LECTURES ON JURISPRUDENCE

YALE LAW SCHOOL · 1938

THE
ADMINISTRATIVE
PROCESS

BY

JAMES M. LANDIS

LUX ET VERITAS

NEW HAVEN AND LONDON
YALE UNIVERSITY PRESS

TO
SAM RAYBURN
OF TEXAS
WHOSE QUIET DESIRE TO SERVE HIS COUNTRY
HAS FASHIONED SO GREATLY THE DEVELOPMENT OF
THE ADMINISTRATIVE PROCESS

CONTENTS

Foreword
Louis L. Jaffe

THE distinguished work of James Landis in administrative law was in some respects a Pilgrim's Progress representative of the "liberal" lawyer's experience during the thirty formative years between 1931 and 1961. "For me," he said in a speech before the Administrative Law Section of the American Bar Association in 1961, "to have watched the growth of the administrative process has been perhaps the most exciting chapter of my life." In his well-known lectures, *The Administrative Process*, delivered in 1938 while Dean of the Harvard Law School, he had assigned a role of preponderant importance to the administrative process and indicated that his mood was one of exuberant optimism:[1]

So much in the way of hope for the regulation of enterprise, for the realization of claims to a better livelihood has, since the turn of the century, been made to rest upon the administrative process. To arm it with the means to effectuate those hopes is but to preserve the current of American living. To leave it powerless to achieve its purposes is to imperil too greatly the things that we have learned to hold dear.

In the years immediately preceding the Landis lectures, the New Deal had enacted and put into vigorous operation the most thoroughgoing program of reform in our history. The social service state ap-

1. Below, p. 122.

Originally published under the title "James Landis and the Administrative Process," in (1964) 78 HARV. L. REV. 319-28.

peared to have arisen as a full-fledged phoenix from
the ashes of the Great Depression. Among its most
spectacular accomplishments were the regulation of
security issues, stock exchanges, and public utility
holding companies, and the enactment of the National Labor Relations Act, the Magna Charta of
organized labor. These programs were administered
by newly established independent agencies. Landis, a
young man of superb intellect and vigor, just recently appointed professor in the Law School, had
been instrumental in drafting the securities and exchange legislation and had served successively as a
member of the Federal Trade Commission, member
of the Securities and Exchange Commission, and
Chairman of the Securities and Exchange Commission, before being appointed Dean of the Law
School. His lectures in 1938 became inevitably a cele-
bration, a defense, and a rationalization of the mag-
nificent accomplishment in which he had played so
brilliant a part. This accounts for their assured air,
their engaging *élan,* as it accounts for what we today
would see as a reading somewhat too cavalier in its
disregard of the teachings of tradition, and somewhat
blind to the truth that tradition speaks not only of
the past but of the future. Yet Landis spoke for all of
us who had been deeply committed to the New Deal
and who had been intimately associated with the administrative process.

At the heart of the lectures there is a master thesis.
The administrative process "is not, as some suppose,
simply an extension of executive power. . . . In the
grant to it of that full ambit of authority necessary
for it in order to plan, to promote, and to police, it

presents an assemblage of rights normally exercisable by government as a whole."[2]

Taking the Interstate Commerce Commission as a model, Landis posited the proposition that what was important was the deliberate organization of a governmental unit whose single concern was the wellbeing, in a public sense, of a vital national industry.[3]

If in private life we were to organize a unit for the operation of an industry, it would scarcely follow Montesquieu's lines. . . . Yet the problems of operating a private industry resemble to a great degree those entailed by its regulation. . . . [W]hen government concerns itself with the stability of an industry it is only intelligent realism for it to follow the industrial rather than the political analogue. . . . The dominant theme in the administrative structure is thus determined not primarily by political conceptualism but rather by concern for an industry whose economic health has become a responsibility of government.[4]

Underlying this thesis was the premise that insofar as *laissez faire* had broken down there arose a need for vesting in a public authority supervision over the economic integrity and normal development of industries.[5] "If the railroads are 'sick' we listen eagerly to what Commissioner Eastman may have to say upon the subject."[6] Railroads were the model of a sick industry, but banking and the stock exchange as well were thought of as problems the solutions of which were the responsibility of the independent agencies[7]

---

2. P. 15.
3. P. 10.
4. Pp. 10-12.
5. P. 16.
6. P. 17.
7. *Ibid.*

to whom would be committed "the initial shaping and
enforcement of industrial policies."[8] The overtones of
this thesis suggested the possibilities of its indefinite
extension. "If the administrative process is to fill the
need for expertness, obviously, as regulation increases, the number of our administrative authorities
must increase. . . . Efficiency in the process of governmental regulation is best served by the creation of
more rather than less agencies."[9]

These concepts and the hopes that they generated
rested, as we can now see, on a misreading—or at best
an oversimplified reading—of the New Deal experience itself, and on a failure to reckon with traditional
truths which despite their platitudinous character are
truths nevertheless. Neither in the past nor under the
New Deal had regulatory agencies planned for the
well-being or normal development of an industry; and
there is little in our experience to indicate that they
are capable of doing so. The ICC's regulation of
transportation had, it is true, become much more
comprehensive over the years, but this meant essentially that its veto power became more comprehensive.
Not only are external veto powers not a prime source
of energy and enterprise, but they create a danger of
stifling the imagination and risk-taking that is essential to progressive industrial action. It was, we must
remember, part of our thinking at that time that the
old order was sick and dying, that it had exhausted its
potentiality. When the railroads were "sick" we were
to call upon Dr. Eastman for remedies. His remedy,
as we know, was more and yet more regulation and less

8. P. 23.
9. P. 24.

and less competition. The irony here was tremendous. It had become an accepted tenet among the right thinking that the ICC was an astounding success, the prime exhibit of the potential of the administrative process. Joseph Eastman had become something of an administrative divinity. One of the "checks" on an agency, argued Landis, was the fact that its policies "must be 'right' from an industrial standpoint"![10] If not, he implies, the agency's exposure and loss of effective credit would be swift. Yet here were the railroads being rushed along the rails to their ruin. Ultimately when they sought to convince the Commission that they should be permitted to cut rates to meet the competition of the trucks and barges they were denied relief in the name of coordination. The nostrum most approved by an administrator for the ills of a regulated industry is more regulation; to him it seems as obvious as to the doctors of another era that the remedy for unsuccessful bleeding is more bleeding. The concern with stability behind the Landis thesis was, of course, an understandable residue of the Great Depression. Yet the experience of the National Industrial Recovery Act with its gigantic bureaucracy of entrenched and monopolistic trade associations might have taught us that the administrative process was not the proper organ for the shaping and enforcement of industrial policies.[11] Brandeis, that old

---

10. P. 99.

11. Landis suggests that the failure of the NIRA was due to "the enormous expanse of its jurisdiction." P. 87. Administrators could not be expected to become experts in so many lines. But would the alternative of as many separate agencies as there are industries have succeeded where the NIRA did not?

preacher of the gospel of *laissez faire*, saw it, but we young ones patronized his quaint wisdom.

Landis was encouraged in the possibilities of planning by his experience on the SEC. The Commission did not always wait for problems to arise in the form of a case or controversy; it looked ahead and prepared itself by investigation and study. But this is not planning the policies of an industry; it is planning the *regulation* of an industry. To do that is clearly feasible and without question one of the most valuable and constructive functions of which an administrative agency is capable.

If we conceive of the administrative agency not as an industrial policymaker but as regulator, Landis's estimate, if it errs on the side of enthusiasm, does nevertheless vividly define its virtues and sagely recognize its potential shortcomings. His analysis, we might say, lacks only one dimension: the dynamic of history. He knows, for example, that an agency's "relative isolation from the popular democratic processes occasionally arouses the antagonism of legislators . . . ";[12] that "the agency must have friends, friends who can give it substantial political assistance . . . ";[13] that it is not possible to delegate to the administrative the responsibility for major decision-making in default of the resolution by the legislative of major power conflicts.[14] And he comes to the very heart of the question when he notes that "the pressing problem today . . . is to get the administrative to assume the responsibilities that it properly should as-

12. P. 50.
13. P. 61.
14. P. 59.

sume. Political and official life to too great an extent tends to favor routinization. The assumption of responsibility by an agency is always a gamble that may well make more enemies than friends. The easiest course is frequently that of inaction."[15] And finally he quotes the observation of Gerard Henderson that " 'the science of administration owes its being to the fact that most government affairs are run by men of average capabilities, and that it is necessary to supply such men with a routine and a ready-made technique. . . .' "[16]

These acute observations add up in essence to the traditional wisdom concerning the routine conservatism of bureaucracies. But they are offered by Landis not to discount his glowing picture of administrative potentiality but rather to spur agencies on to even greater accomplishments and to secure for them the fullest measure of power to overcome these latent threats to their effective action. We must recall once again that our generation—that of Landis and myself —judged the administrative process in terms of its stunning performance under the New Deal. We did not in our estimate take into account the unique concatenation of circumstances which made for that performance: the desperate panic of the people; the terrible shock to the confidence and prestige of those who had held power; the rush into the vacuum of a whole phalanx of talented, passionate, exasperated, deprived men, those who for years had been clamoring for reform, and those who were their disciples. These men had ready an enormous, articulated backlog of

15. P. 75.
16. P. 41.

tasks long overdue, tasks pent up, waiting to be achieved. These were the galvanic forces that brought the New Deal legislation into being and stoked the high fires of its administration.

It is too easy now to see that the normal, everyday potential of the administrative process could not be evaluated in terms of its New Deal performance. Given those circumstances it was a splendid instrument. The latter-day critics of the administrative process who measure its capabilities in terms of its performance and the claims made for it in the days of the New Deal have less excuse for their lack of perspective. The administrative agency whether independent or not continues to be a valuable tool of government. There are many day-to-day tasks that cannot be otherwise performed. Give an agency a decently defined mandate, adequate funds, its due quota of "men of average capabilities" and it will do a good job; in its way, as good as, let us say, Congress, the judiciary, and the run-of-the-mill executive bureaucracies. From time to time, such an agency will be given a new job—a job intensely desired by a significant element of the community and adequately mandated by the legislature; with its streamlined, multifaceted power it may accomplish a breakthrough, as did the Labor Board and the SEC. I do not think, however, that the administrative agency has—as contrasted with what Landis would call the executive— a unique power for achieving reform or giving direction to our economy. Taxation, fiscal policy, contracting, grants-in-aid may be as powerful, perhaps far more powerful, movers and shakers.

Finally, even when regulation is the appropriate

means of reform, students of government have no warrant for the view that an administrative agency can be expected to put into effect a program of continuous reform, that is, to resolve novel conflicts without a new legislative mandate. Basic reform is not a matter of technique or expertise. It calls for a redistribution of power; only the legislative and the executive branches can hammer out the resolution of major power conflicts. Those, for example, who lecture the FCC are, for the most part, directing their exhortations to the wrong audience.

Neither the education nor contribution of Landis ended with his 1938 lectures. Appointed to an unexpired term in 1946, he served for over a year as Chairman of the Civil Aeronautics Board. He was not reappointed. I believe that he attributed the failure of reappointment to opposition by the airlines. This, of course, was in shocking contrast to his New Deal experience, and it taught him that the administrative process is as vulnerable as any other part of government. For one who had looked to the administrative process with such exalted expectations, it must have been a peculiarly bitter experience. It was all the worse that in this case the failure was not a failure of a distinguished candidate to present himself but a refusal to use the high talent of one eager to serve. But, of course, the two sides of the equation tend to come into equilibrium; the prospect of such capricious refusal of reappointment discourages the worthy nonpolitical aspirant. When finally in 1960 Landis was to advise President-elect Kennedy on ways and means to strengthen the administrative process he emphasized the improvement of top personnel. His suggestions ran along two closely related lines: first, changes in the laws to make the jobs more attractive; second, better appointment practices.[17] Commissioners should be persons of skill and experience in business, law, engineering, or other professions. Persons of this caliber will usually have established themselves on a permanent basis in financial terms, present or prospective, considerably beyond government salaries. Even assuming that such a person has a strong sense of public spirit and that the job has prestige (which, under current conditions, is not always the case), there is a limit to the risk and sacrifice he will wish to take. If he thinks of the job as a career, he faces a short tenure (five to seven years) and the lack of a tradition of reappointment. If he has in mind no more than a meritorious or advantageous interlude, the financial problem arises not only from the possible salary cut, but from the costs of liquidating investments, moving his family, and special entertaining.

Landis believed that the central problem was the short and uncertain tenure. He did not believe that a salary increase of $2,500 to $5,000 would make much difference. But he did suggest a moderate entertainment allowance so that a Commissioner could entertain rather than be required to suffer entertainment (the latter today creates suspicion of improper influence). He recommended also an adequate retirement allowance. Even more important, I would suppose, for those contemplating a limited tour of duty, is making less rigorous the requirement of liquidating

---

17. See generally Landis, *Report on Regulatory Agencies to the President-elect* (Senate Comm. on the Judiciary, 86th Cong., 1st Sess., Comm. Print 1960).

investments. As to tenure, Landis advocated an increase to ten years. Life tenure would probably not be
politically feasible and would not, perhaps, be advisable for one exercising power "in these areas of dynamic activity."[18] But these changes will only make
matters worse if appointments are based not on competence but on politics. Landis was surely on sound
ground in calling for improved methods and practices
of recruitment. But I am afraid that we must not
expect too much improvement here. As Gerard Henderson warned us, we must not on the average hope
for better than men of "average capabilities."

Even as late as 1960 an attitude of limited expectations ran contrary, if not to the teaching of his
experience, at least to his expressed thinking. In his
recommendations to Kennedy, Landis still spoke with
the optimistic voice of the forward-looking academic
and lawyer of the great decades of the twenties and
the thirties. These were the times when the most
brilliant legal scholars under the banner of realism
were shattering the absolutes that stood guard over
the Old World. Many of them taught, indeed, that
rules and precepts were illusion; the law by its very
nature could never be other than a congeries of specific incidents responsive to "reality." But their reality was itself a construct based on new concepts;
their motivation was the destruction of the old to
make way for the new. Their successes both in private
and public law have been and continue to be impres-
sive. Landis was deeply impregnated with this philos-

---

18. The recommendations in this paragraph may be found in *id.*
at 66-68.

ophy and with the more general master premise of Pound that the law must first define the job to be done and then "engineer" the proper instruments for doing it. It was this philosophy that led Landis to begin his scholarly career with the systematic study of legislation and made his famous article, "Statutes and the Sources of Law,"[19] his single greatest contribution to the law.

Nowhere are his great expectations more vividly implied than in his dramatic recital of the failures of the agencies to "plan" the solution of a whole array of great problems in the fields of transportation, communications, energy, monopoly, and unfair trade practices, with its implication that by adopting the appropriate procedures the agencies can in the future succeed where they have until now failed.[20] These failures in his opinion resulted from technical failures of two sorts. They first are operational failures within the agency. An agency is apt to concentrate upon the day-to-day litigation docket with a corresponding absence of policy "planning." Furthermore, (as has also been emphasized by Lewis Hector and Newton Minow) it has become fairly common for an agency to formulate policy and rules as it would conduct litigation, that is, to comply with the full complement of litigatory procedural apparatus. Both Hector and Minow would have divorced the adjudicatory and rule (policy) functions, assigning the latter to an officer operating under the aegis of the executive and using informal administrative procedures. But Landis

---

19. In *Harvard Legal Essays Written in Honor of Joseph Henry Beale and Samuel Williston* (1934), p. 213.

20. Landis, supra note 17, at 22-24. See generally *id.* at 15-35.

would still combine these functions. It has, in his opinion, the advantage of mutual reinforcement. With adequate delegation, he believed, the top personnel can find the time for planning. The second type of failure is the failure of coordination among agencies having responsibilities in a common area. Professors and students of public administration have consistently opposed the "independent" regulatory agency insofar as it is used as an instrument of major policymaking. Policy powers in their opinion must be exercised under the executive if they are to be exercised coherently and to win political acceptance. The professors have spoken of the agencies as a "headless fourth branch." In his 1938 lectures Landis ridiculed this criticism, particularly the figure of speech used to express it. It was, he said, hysterical. "Its sweeping condemnation of the process seems to proceed almost upon the mystical hypothesis that the number 'four' bespeaks evil or waste as contrasted with some beneficence emanating from the number 'three.' "[21] It is always dangerous, of course, to use a vivid figure of speech; one's critics will do logical mayhem upon it without directing themselves to the underlying thought. But in his report to the President, Landis had become acutely aware of the need for coordinating policy planning at the highest level. He still held to the view that the so-called "independence" of the agencies was of little relevance in this connection. Their independence is so tenuous, he thought, that it hardly stands in the way of any real presidential demand for coordination; and on the

21. Below, p. 47.

other hand, in the absence of actual pressure from the President himself (which can only rarely be exercised) the executive agencies will just as effectively resist coordination. There is, I think, considerable truth in this estimate. But I think the truth goes also to prove that regardless of organization, coordination in complex controversial areas is very hard to achieve.

I would suggest that with our vast, many-purposed bureaucracy headed by an overburdened President and Congress, we cannot hope that institutional arrangements will be able, simply because we have identified a problem, to provide a well-coordinated attack. It is not enough to point out that the transportation problem requires a coordinated effort. It is not enough to set up multiagency committees. It is not enough to suggest, as did Landis, that there be established in the Executive Office of the President offices for Communications, Transportation, Energy, and "Oversight of Regulatory Agencies" "with authority to propose to the President plans," and so on, and to "assist the President in discharging his responsibility of assuring the efficient execution" of the laws administered by the regulatory agencies.[22] I do not wish to be misunderstood. I am not asserting that we cannot devise machinery for settling problems, great, medium, and small. What I am suggesting is that we cannot devise a machinery that will solve problems requiring the exercise of power as soon as the problems become "visible." Normally a failure of coordination among officers having responsibility

---

22. Landis, supra note 17, at 85-86.

in a common area (Congressmen, President, executive officials, bureaucrats, independent authorities) manifests an underlying conflict of interests for which it has not as yet been possible to secure a consensus. The reasons for the absence of consensus may be one or all of the following: (a) the priority of other tasks; (b) the wealth and influence of those interested in the *status quo;* (c) the weakness of those who seek to change it (for example, the narrow intelligentsia that alone is concerned with the character and quality of TV); (d) the more or less equal power of the opposing forces; (e) the inability to make a convincing analysis or to devise an apparently effective solution.

If I thus emphasize the difficulties, it is only to suggest that there are no grand institutional solutions that will enable us simultaneously to put in order all of the problem areas. But this does not warrant a hostile attitude toward innovation. It is only by persistent trial and error that we may hope to gain on our problems. Throughout the last thirty years there has been a remarkable flow of constructive criticism and administrative creativity. Landis was in the forefront of those whose intellect and vigor were committed to the task of continuous regeneration.

THE ADMINISTRATIVE PROCESS

INTRODUCTION

THE last century has witnessed the rise of a new instrument of government, the administrative tribunal. In its mature form it is difficult to find its parallels in our earlier political history; its development seems indigenous. The rapidity of its growth, the significance of its powers, and the implications of its being, are such as to require notice of the extent to which this new "administrative law" is weaving itself more and more into our governmental fabric.

In terms of political theory, the administrative process springs from the inadequacy of a simple tripartite form of government to deal with modern problems. It represents a striving to adapt governmental technique, that still divides under three rubrics, to modern needs and, at the same time, to preserve those elements of responsibility and those conditions of balance that have distinguished Anglo-American government.

Separation of powers as a political maxim is old; but as a principle of government, sanctified by being elevated to the constitutional level and embroidered by pontifical moral phrases, it has a distinctly American flavor. Our British cousins discover it now and then as they find that its preachment fits some practical or political need. But it was left to us to hallow the tripartite ideal of government, wherein all power delegated by the people was in the purported interests of liberty divided neatly between legislative, executive, and judicial. It was left to us, moreover, not merely to make of this division a convenient way of thinking about government, of considering the desirability of checking and balancing a particular power that might be vested in some official or some body, but also by judicial introspection to distinguish minutely and definitively between these powers. That fineness of logic-chopping that characterizes our courts permits us at will to discern a legislative or a judicial power when we are eager for a determination; at the same time it permits us to avoid decision by the establishment of new categories of quasi-legislative and quasi-judicial powers.

The insistence upon the compartmentalization of power along triadic lines gave way in the nineteenth century to the exigencies of governance. Without too much political theory but with a keen sense of the practicalities of the situation, agencies were created whose functions embraced the three aspects of government. Rule-making, enforcement, and the disposition of competing claims made by contending parties, were all intrusted to them. As the years passed, the process grew. These agencies, tribunals, and rule-making boards were for the sake of convenience distinguished from the existing governmental bureaucracies by terming them "administrative." The law the courts permitted them to make was named "administrative law," so that now the process in all its component parts can be appropriately termed the "administrative process."

The terminology, like the formulation of the doctrine of the separation of powers, seems to have had a Gallic origin. In 1914 Dicey evinced concern over

the fact that due to certain "statutes passed under
the influence of socialistic ideas" the law of England
was beginning to exhibit certain characteristics of
the French *droit administratif*.[1] In 1885 he had advanced the belief that those tendencies were funda-
mentally inconsistent with English traditions and
customs and therefore could not logically inhere in
English law.[2] But in 1915, after the decision of the
House of Lords in *Local Government Board* v. *Ar-
lidge*,[3] he was more than ever convinced that the
qualification which he had been forced to place upon
his 1885 views was now corroborated; and once again
he likened the "novel" happenings in England to
prevailing conditions in France.[4] Because *droit administratif* concerned the disposition of claims between the government and the individual, and because
the major emphasis of our newer administrative
agencies appeared to concern the same category of
claims, a superficial similarity was present. Moreover, the term "administrative law" had had neither
analytic nor historical definition. It was thus easy to
employ it to describe governmental law-making and
law enforcement by agencies that for one reason or
another fail to submit to convenient classification
within one of the three historic branches of government.

Naming is significant. Not only does it permit one
to point to a thing or a thought, but, as Stuart Chase
has told us, leads us thereby to invest a thing or a

---

1. Dicey, *Law of the Constitution* (8th ed., 1923), p. xliv.
2. *Id.,* chap. XII.   3. [1915] A.C. 120.
4. Dicey, *Development of Administrative Law in England*
(1915) 31 L.Q.REV. 148.

thought with properties attached to the object theretofore associated with the name. How true this is of
the administrative process is evident by reference to
the voluminous literature upon the subject. *Droit
administratif*, being the system of law and courts
that dealt with the claims of the individual against
government, to the English mind bespoke bureaucracy. The term administrative law had thus the same
emphasis. From bureaucracy to autocracy to dicta-
torship is a simple transition. And that transition
has frequently been made in the literature of the administrative process. That literature abounds with
fulmination. It treats the administrative process as
if it were an antonym of that supposedly immemorial
and sacred right of every Englishman, the legal pal-
ladium of "the rule of law." The process is denounced
by worthy lawyers and others as heralding the death
knell of ancient liberties and privileges. Only a year
ago a distinguished group of scholars, reporting to
the President of the United States—in language
hardly indicative of academic restraint—described
the independent administrative agencies of the federal government as constituting "a headless 'fourth
branch' of the Government, a haphazard deposit of
irresponsible agencies and uncoördinated powers,"
whose institution did "violence to the basic theory of
the American Constitution that there should be three
major branches of the Government and only three."[5]

Such apotheosizing obscures rather than clarifies
thought. Despite this chorus of abuse and tirade, the

5. *Administrative Management in the Government of the United
States, The President's Committee on Administrative Management*
(1937), p. 36.

growth of the administrative process shows little sign of being halted. Instead, it still exhibits the vigor that attends lusty youth, and, if we have defined our subject rightly, it is a youth with which we are concerned. For here is an institution that has existed for less than a century and which, with a few exceptions, has been of public moment for only a little more than half that time. Yet, its extraordinary growth in recent years, the increasing frequency with which government has come to resort to it, the extent to which it is creating new relationships between the individual, the body economic, and the state, already have given it great stature. An expansive analysis of that process is beyond my present scope. More appropriate, at this time, is a preliminary inquiry into its origins, an examination of its nature, and an appraisal of its potentialities as a technique for dealing with modern problems.

I. THE PLACE OF THE ADMINISTRATIVE TRIBUNAL

AT the turn of the nineteenth century the functions of government were limited essentially to the prevention of disorder, protection from foreign invasion, the enlargement of national boundaries, the stimulation of international trade, and the creation of a scheme of officials to settle civil disputes. These functions required men and facilities for their performance, and thus the maintenance of this officialdom made the collection of revenue a matter of persistent concern. In the field of taxation and that of police, we find the normal incidence of claims by government against the individual.

The correction of the breach of regulations in these fields could not be left to the initiative of the particular individual involved. Government had to assume the part of plaintiff or prosecutor. The individual's whim, his lack of financial ability to prosecute his claim, could not be made the determinants of the social policy that should be the fact of living as distinguished from the policy that might theoretically be a part of the common law or that might have the verbal blessing of the legislature. In these fields government thus had to assume the initiative in calling for the visitation of such penalties that the law of the day might impose for infractions. In the jurisprudential language of today we are accustomed to talk of great social interests underlying the prosecution of these claims; accustomed, too, to note how as time advanced these social interests increased and so made the protection of additional claims the direct concern of government. This is, of course, simply a rationalization of the growing interdependence of individuals in our civilization and the consequent necessity of insisting upon the observation of rules of conduct. It is the fact of interdependence that is the warp for such rationalization, and it is that fact rather than the weft of rationalization that accounts today for the administrative process.

Two tendencies in the expanding civilization of the late nineteenth century seem to me to foreshadow the need for methods of government different in kind from those that had prevailed in the past. These are the rise of industrialism and the rise of democracy. Naturally, these two tendencies combined and interacted each upon the other, so that it becomes difficult to isolate cause and effect. For as a dynamic society does not move *in vacuo,* so an abstract classification of tendencies can have only a relative value. The rise of industrialism and the rise of democracy, however, brought new and difficult problems to government. A world that scarcely a hundred years ago could listen to Wordsworth's denunciation of railroads because their building despoiled the beauty of his northern landscapes is different, very different, from one that in 1938 has to determine lanes and flight levels for air traffic. While it was true that advances in transportation, communication, and mass production were in themselves disturbing elements, the profound problems were the social and economic questions that flowed from the era of mechanical invention. To their solution some contribution derived from the rise of humanitarianism. But the driving force was the rec-

ognition by the governing classes of our civilization
of their growing dependence upon the promotion of
the welfare of the governed. Concessions to rectify
social maladjustments thus had to be made, however
grudgingly. And as the demands for positive solutions increased and, in the form of legislative measures, were precipitated upon the cathodes of governmental activity, *laissez faire*—the simple belief that
only good could come by giving economic forces free
play—came to an end.

This industrial development coincided with basic
shifts in the sources of governmental power. The Reform Bill of 1832 in England, the abolition of property qualifications on the right of suffrage in this
country, Jacksonism and its implications, all pres-
aged the stirring of new and powerful forces. There
grows a conception of government as the concern of
the common man; politics as the means whereby he
may realize the dream of a better living. At first the
conception is narrow. It manifests itself in the desire
for sporadic intervention on the part of government
to adjust a particular abuse. But later it expands
into a view which conceives it to be a function of government to maintain a continuing concern with and
control over the economic forces which affect the life
of the community. These forces are recognized to be
more or less permanently at play; but, unfortunately,
they seem either to lack direction and objective or to
have objectives differing from those desired by the
newer elements that have now become part of the
sources of governmental power. It is these developments that political commentators at the turn of the
century pointed to as illustrative of collectivistic and

socialistic forces prevalent in government. However accurate the use of that terminology may have been, it was no doubt a fact that government was responding to the demands of new pressures at the source of its authority. More and more the state was assuming new burdens in order to direct and to define the objectives of the economic forces that invention had released, and to control the new powers that derived from the wealth which those forces had created.

These forces can be traced by their concrete manifestations in the growth and forms of the administrative process. The high level of transportation charges and the existence of tariffs that discriminated between communities, commodities, and individuals had made the railroads a political issue. The first attempts at a direct legislative control of rates and charges proved crude and useless. Such remedies as the common law and the courts afforded depended upon the initiative of aggrieved shippers. In effect they were more apparent than real because of the costly and uncertain character of the legal actions that had to be pursued. The need for nondiscriminatory and reasonable rates, uniformly applicable, could not be achieved through the intermittent intervention of the judicial process. The problem was plainly seen to transcend state boundaries when in 1886 the Supreme Court of the United States by its decision in *Wabash Ry. Co.* v. *Illinois*[1] removed three fourths of the railway tonnage from the potential control of the states.[2] Some federal mechanism of

1. 118 U.S. 557 (1886).
2. See Sharfman, *The Interstate Commerce Commission* (1931), I, 19.

necessity had to be invented if the rudiments of a national railroad policy were to be developed.

More important than the immediate powers that in 1887 were vested in the Interstate Commerce Commission was the creation of the Commission itself. A government had to be provided to direct and control an industry, and governance as a practical matter implied not merely legislative power or simply executive power, but whatever power might be required to achieve the desired results. It is not too important to our purposes that in 1887 the powers granted to the Interstate Commerce Commission were meager and that the objectives for which they had been created were of themselves limited. Political pressures, remnants of *laissez faire* economics, the moneyed interests of the East, all made for these limitations. The necessary powers were granted later when the need for them could no longer be denied. What was important was the deliberate organization of a governmental unit whose single concern was the well-being, in a broad public sense, of a vital and national industry.

If in private life we were to organize a unit for the operation of an industry, it would scarcely follow Montesquieu's lines. As yet no organization in private industry either has been conceived along those triadic contours, nor would its normal development, if so conceived, have tended to conform to them. Yet the problems of operating a private industry resemble to a great degree those entailed by its regulation. The direction of any large corporation presents difficulties comparable in character to those faced by an administrative commission. Rates are a concern, likewise wages, hours of employment, safe conditions for labor, and schemes for pensions and gratuities. There must follow the enforcement of pertinent regulations as well as the adjudication of claims of every nature made not only by employees but also by the public. This is in fact governance. It is true that the sanctions available to the governing bodies of industry to enforce decisions differ from those traditionally employed by government; but, partly because of the rapidity and directness of their execution, the penalties that private management can impose possess a coercive force and effect that government even with its threat of incarceration cannot equal. The management of a business like the United States Steel Corporation has wide powers to affect the economic security, stability, and subsistence level of its two hundred thousand employees. It has power, too, to influence the lives of its numberless customers. But more than this, such a corporation either by itself or in combination with its contemporaries can virtually determine what policies with reference to the production and sale of steel we shall pursue as a nation.

The significance of this comparison is not that it may point to a need for an expanding concept of the province of governmental regulation, but rather that it points to the form which governmental action tends to take. As the governance of industry, bent upon the shaping of adequate policies and the development of means for their execution, vests powers to this end without regard to the creation of agencies theoretically independent of each other, so when government concerns itself with the stability of an industry it is only intelligent realism for it to follow the industrial rather than the political analogue. It vests the necessary powers with the administrative authority it creates, not too greatly concerned with the extent to which such action does violence to the traditional tripartite theory of governmental organization. The dominant theme in the administrative structure is thus determined not primarily by political conceptualism but rather by concern for an industry whose economic health has become a responsibility of government.

In the history of the Interstate Commerce Commission these developments are clearly visible. In 1903 the railroads themselves brought about the enactment of the Elkins Act to provide more effective means in preventing departures from the published tariffs.[3] Again in 1906 the jurisdiction of the Commission was broadened to embrace other facilities of transportation such as express companies, sleeping car companies, and pipe lines. These were so integrated with the railroad problem as to make effective adoption of a unified industrial policy impossible without their inclusion. Similarly, the desirability of a reasonable rate structure having now been conceded, the right to bring it into existence was given to the Commission.[4] Further powers were granted in 1910 and here, too, there was first manifested a concern over the need for coördinating financial and operating policies.[5] The experience of the World War

3. Sharfman, *op. cit.*, p. 36.   4. *Id.*, chap. I, § 4.
5. For the report of the so-called Hadley Commission, appointed by President Taft pursuant to the authority granted by the Mann-Elkins Act of 1910, see House Doc. No. 256, 62d Cong. 2d Sess. (1911).

made more acute than ever the necessity for wider powers of control, powers to foster as well as to proscribe. In the Transportation Act of 1920 we find not only a reappraisal of earlier policies and a further extension of powers, but a distinct affirmation of the requirement of a more comprehensive, more responsible national railroad policy. It is at this stage that the powers granted to the Commission clearly illustrate their conformity to the industrial rather than the political pattern. In their essentials they resemble the powers conferred upon the executive committee of a board of directors in the hope of building a system which, under the guidance of this committee, may more nearly approximate a given desideratum. Thenceforth, as responsibility for the efficient functioning of the railroads is assumed in greater degree by the nation, the Commission possesses less the appearance of a tribunal and more that of a committee charged with the task of achieving the best possible operation of the railroads.

This assumption by the Interstate Commerce Commission of a wider responsibility reflects itself in the public utterances of its outstanding members. These men, as they now view their duties, are no longer content to base the justification of their stewardship upon achievements that merely assure reasonable rates and the absence of discrimination. Instead the ills of the industry have become their bailiwick. The policies they must formulate must now be directed toward broad and imaginative ends, conceived in terms of management rather than of police.

In the years that followed the creation of the Interstate Commerce Commission, the same problem presented itself at other points in the economic scene. As particular industries, due to lack of effective economic restraints, posited problems of abusive tactics with which traditional legal devices had failed to cope, this new method of control made its appearance. Banking, insurance, utilities, shipping, communications—industries with sicknesses stemming from misdirection as to objective or from failure adequately to meet public needs—all came under the fostering guardianship of the state. The mode of the exercise of that guardianship was the administrative process.

Following the economic breakdown of 1929, a perplexed state relied almost entirely upon the administrative approach to its many and staggering problems. As rapidly as—indeed, sometimes more rapidly than—causes could be isolated and problems defined, administrative agencies were created to wrestle with them. Many of these were frankly temporary in character, hastily set up to cope with emergency situations. Some were later discarded, others evolved into more enduring institutions. Among the permanent regulatory efforts was that of securities regulation. More rapidly than in the case of the Interstate Commerce Commission, administrative grappling with this problem passed through the simple concern of police to considerations pertinent to the public well-being of an industry. Beginning in 1933 with the requirement for disclosure as a condition precedent to the public offering of new securities, there was added in 1934 to the responsibilities of government the correction of abuses in trading in outstanding securi-

ties. In the same year these two regulative statutes
were intrusted to the care of a newly created administrative commission. It soon became apparent that
regulation in this field implied the governance of
what is essentially an industry consisting of investment banker, broker, and dealer. As in the case of the
Interstate Commerce Commission, it was not long before it became evident that the mere proscription of
abuses was insufficient to effect the realization of the
broad objectives that lay behind the movement for
securities legislation. The primary emphasis of administrative activity had to center upon the guidance
and supervision of the industry as a whole. Its re-
orientation and reorganization have, in consequence,
occupied more effort, more vigor, and more foresight
on the part of the administrative than its activity in
the field of police. And today such efforts continue to
be that agency's chief concern.

Viewed from this standpoint, it is obvious that the
resort to the administrative process is not, as some
suppose, simply an extension of executive power.
Confused observers have sought to liken this development to a pervasive use of executive power. But the
administrative differs not only with regard to the
scope of its powers; it differs most radically in regard to the responsibility it possesses for their exercise. In the grant to it of that full ambit of authority
necessary for it in order to plan, to promote, and to
police, it presents an assemblage of rights normally
exercisable by government as a whole. Moreover, its
characteristic is this concept of governance, limited,
of course, within those boundaries derived from its
constituent statutory authority. But administrative

power, though it may begin as an effort to adapt and make efficient police protection within a particular field, moves soon to think in terms of the economic well-being of an industry. The creation of that power is, in essence, the response made in the light of a tripartite political theory to the demand that government assume responsibility not merely to maintain ethical levels in the economic relations of the members of society, but to provide for the efficient functioning of the economic processes of the state.

A survey of existing administrative agencies reveals how they were called into being when the political power of our democratic institutions found it necessary to exercise some control over the varying phases of our economic life. The many characteristic illustrations that the field affords demonstrate this primary administrative thesis; namely, the existence of a growing need for vesting in a public authority supervision over the economic integrity of industries and their normal development. It is significant to note this trend in the development of the administrative process; it is equally significant to note departures from it. For, indeed, administrative agencies have been created whose jurisdiction related less to a particular type of industrial activity than to a general social and economic problem which cut across a vast number of businesses and occupations.

Typical of this type of administrative agency are the Federal Trade Commission and the National Labor Relations Board. Both have as their jurisdiction the general problem of unfair practices, in the one case as these relate to business and in the other to labor. There was no prototype in the industrial world after which such agencies could be modeled. The lines of their creation as well as the limits upon their activity thus may be seen to diverge considerably from the other type of agency. For both of them are primarily interested from a particular standpoint in the policing of industry as a whole, rather than being vested with supervision over the welfare of a definable line of business. From a popular standpoint they do not represent an authority capable of being held responsible for developments in a particular industry. When today we think of the railroad problem, the banking problem, the stock exchange problem, we think of them in terms of the responsibility for their solution as it may rest with the Interstate Commerce Commission, the Federal Reserve Board, or the Securities and Exchange Commission. If the railroads are "sick" we listen eagerly to what Commissioner Eastman may have to say upon the subject. We desire to know what the Commission of which he is a member can or intends to do about the situation. But in the case of the Federal Trade Commission or the National Labor Relations Board it is otherwise, for neither fulfils a similar task nor bears a like responsibility. Rather they possess more nearly the character of tribunals, of business and labor courts, where the function is one more closely akin to policing as distinguished from promoting.

The distinction is significant. From it may flow some basis for differentiation in the nature and composition of administrative agencies and in their relationship to the other branches of government. Some broad philosophical answer to these questions seems almost imperative now that the administrative process has grown to such proportions. Of that growth in England a distinguished English judge, Lord Macmillan, has recently had this to say:

In contrast with former times Parliament now concerns itself with the regulation of the lives of the people from the cradle—indeed, even ante-natally—to the grave, and being unable itself to deal with all the details it delegates to the government departments the task of carrying out its policy by means of innumerable Statutory Rules and Orders. The most recent statistics (1933, Cmd. 4460) show that whereas the national expenditure under the Acts falling within this category was, in England, in 1900, £31,703,000, the figure for 1931 (or latest available year) was £429,854,000.[6]

Or, to take another standard of measurement, in 1921 Mr. Carr in his lectures on delegated legislation adverted to the quantity of administrative regulations promulgated annually in England. He said:

In mere bulk, the child now dwarfs the parent. Last year while 82 acts of Parliament were placed on the Statute Book, more than ten times as many "statutory rules and orders" of a public character were officially registered under the Rules Publication Act. The annual volume of public general statutes for 1920 occupies less than 600 pages; the two volumes of statutory rules and orders for the same period occupy about five times as many.[7]

In this country, to deal with the federal administrative agencies alone, we have no accurate figures even as to their number. Estimates have varied from 50 to 115, depending upon the viewpoint of the esti-

6. Macmillan, *Local Government Law and Administration in England and Wales* (1934), I, xi.
7. Carr, *Delegated Legislation* (1921), p. 2.

mator as to what may or may not constitute an administrative agency. The output of regulations has never been subjected to measurement, although the published rules and regulations have been said to "cover altogether about eight or ten times as many pages as the Acts passed by Congress."[8] The decisions of those authorities which exercise "judicial powers" are said to be "several times as numerous as the recorded decisions of all the Federal judicial courts."[9]

Some better understanding of the elements which together constitute the concept embracing "administrative agency" or "administrative tribunal" is needed not only to reconcile these variations but to refine our own thinking on the problem. At the outset we can eliminate from that concept those agencies that are, in essence, merely courts. The only excuse for terming them administrative is that they fail to conform exactly to the legal idea of courts as that idea has been distilled by the judges out of Article III of the Constitution. The judges have forced us, as a legal matter, to distinguish in our thinking about "courts," between constitutional courts, legislative courts, and administrative courts. Because, for example, the Supreme Court of the District of Columbia was vested with powers to amend or modify rates established by the Public Utilities Commission of the District, in exercising that jurisdiction, according to the Supreme Court of the United States, it was not exercising "judicial power," the only func-

8. Blachly and Oatman, *Administrative Legislation and Adjudication* (1934), p. 11.
9. *Ibid.*

tion that can properly be exercised by a constitutional court.[10] A legislative court, such as the Supreme Court of the District of Columbia, could be invested by Congress with "legislative power" because under the Constitution the Congress had plenary power in the territory that comprised the District. It could create a court that was not necessarily limited to the exercise of "judicial power." But, inasmuch as this Court also disposes of ordinary controversies in a manner similar to that of a normal court, to this extent it was the repository of the "judicial power" of the Constitution, and hence a constitutional court, the salary of whose members could not be reduced by the Congress.[11] Legal sophistication of this character has led some commentators to classify agencies such as the Board of Tax Appeals, the Court of Customs and Patent Appeals, and even the Court of Claims as "administrative tribunals." But distinctions that relate merely to the inviolability of judicial salaries, the absence of life tenure for judges, the power and tendency to apply different and more flexible procedural rules, the right to admit and consider evidence that would be rejected under a strict application of common law principles, all seem insufficient to alter the essential fact that the agency is still a court that is "passively" adjudicating the merits of such conflicting claims as may be presented to it.

10. Keller v. Potomac Electric Power Co., 261 U.S. 428 (1923).
11. O'Donoghue v. United States, 289 U.S. 516 (1933). The Court of Claims, however, does not fall within the category of constitutional courts. Williams v. United States, 289 U.S. 553 (1933). See, generally, Katz, *Federal Legislative Courts* (1930) 43 Harv.L.Rev. 894; (1933) 43 Yale L.J. 316.

It may be necessary, too, to exclude another long list of agencies from our consideration for the purpose of permitting some fruitful generalizations. These are agencies which outwardly resemble an administrative tribunal but whose functions, like those of a comptroller or a personnel officer in private industry, are concerned with the internal management of the government. In order to provide some safeguard against political pressures, the so-called independent commission form has frequently been adopted as the basis for their organization—as, for example, in the case of both the Civil Service Commission and the United States Employees' Compensation Commission.[12] But the prime functions of such agencies relate to the maintenance and compensation of the governmental service. Such rules and regulations as they promulgate are of a nature comparable to rules prescribed by any official in a private industry whose duties pertain to supervision over the hiring, dismissal, or compensation of employees.

It would seem wise, moreover, to exclude in a general way those proprietary agencies of government that were set up for the conduct of a particular enterprise. Into this classification would fall bodies such as the Tennessee Valley Authority, the Reconstruction Finance Corporation, and the Electric Home and Farm Authority. Usually these agencies assume the corporate form, but the mere fact that particular powers may be exercised through that form does not mean that the purposes for which the

12. The duties of the United States Employees' Compensation Commission extend to the administration of the Longshoremen's and Harbor Workers' Compensation Act, 33 U.S.C. c.18, § 939.

authority has been created are thereby outside the field of governmental regulation. Sanctions by way of denial or grant of a privilege, as in the case of the Federal Deposit Insurance Corporation, can be equally as effective as a resort to punitive measures.

Eliminating these types of authorities still leaves a range of administrative agencies characterized by an extraordinary diversity of methods and objective. For agencies may differ in respect of the tenure of their officials, the measure of their independence, their relationship to the courts, their powers to investigate and prosecute, and in a hundred and one other details. The effort to run a rational unifying thread through these bodies at first seems impossible. Certainly the effort to correlate and integrate them according to whether or not they happen to be independent is, to say the least, sterile. The lack of independence results sometimes from political maneuvering rather than from a deliberate theory of creation. The present executive attempt to organize them about the kernel of independence[13] can serve, at best, a very limited purpose, for little common ground of any substance can be visualized as existing between the Works Progress Administration and the Federal Trade Commission, the National Youth Administration and the Interstate Commerce Commission, the Bituminous Coal Commission and the Civilian Conservation Corps.

When we come to the more significant agencies it

13. See *New York Times,* Oct. 22, 1937, p. 1. Eighteen establishments were embraced in this effort "to bring about a closer coordination of efforts . . . and to prevent the overlapping of duties and jurisdictions which frequently arise in the farflung activities of the government."

will be seen that they have as the central theme of their activity either the orderly supervision of a specific industry or, as in the case of the Federal Trade Commission, an extension of a particular branch of the police work of the general government. Their tasks are regulatory, it is true, but, with certain exceptions, regulatory in a broad sense, for to them is committed the initial shaping and enforcement of industrial policies.

The advantages of specialization in the field of regulatory activity seem obvious enough. But our governmental organization of the nineteenth century proceeded upon a different theory. Indeed, theorists have lifted the inexpertness that characterized our nineteenth-century governmental mechanisms to the level of a political principle. Such a practical politician as Andrew Jackson took occasion to urge the Congress to take measures against permitting the civil servants of the government a "long continuance" in office.[14] But expertness cannot derive otherwise. It springs only from that continuity of interest, that ability and desire to devote fifty-two weeks a year, year after year, to a particular problem. With the rise of regulation, the need for expertness became dominant; for the art of regulating an industry requires knowledge of the details of its operation, ability to shift requirements as the condition of

14. President Jackson in his first message to Congress concluded his observations upon this topic with the following recommendation: "I submit, therefore, to your consideration whether the efficiency of the Government would not be promoted and official industry and integrity better served by a general extension of the law which limits appointments to four years." Richardson, *Messages and Papers of the Presidents,* II, 449.

the industry may dictate, the pursuit of energetic measures upon the appearance of an emergency, and the power through enforcement to realize conclusions as to policy.

If the administrative process is to fill the need for expertness, obviously, as regulation increases, the number of our administrative authorities must increase. The most superficial criticism which can be directed toward the development of the administrative process is that which bases its objections merely upon numerical growth. A consequence of an expanding interest of government in various phases of the industrial scene must be the creation of more administrative agencies if the demand for expertness is to be met. Increasing their number of itself need not disturb us, provided that the relationships between them, and in turn their relationship to the other departments of government, are properly solved. Efficiency in the processes of governmental regulation is best served by the creation of more rather than less agencies. And it is efficiency that is the desperate need.

In the public discussion and debate of today, a curious paradox is evident. There is currently strong objection to the vertical integration that in many fields characterizes modern industrial development. There is widespread distrust of a tendency for business to become so large as to demand more in the way of management than may be reasonably expected of the average human intelligence. But at the same time we find a converse tendency when discussion turns to the administrative side of government. Not infrequently little hesitation attends the projection of government into a vast new field of action; but bitter altercation develops as soon as the suggestion is made that responsibility for the execution of these new duties be placed in the hands of a select, compact group of individuals. The creation of any new administrative agency is viewed always with regret and frequently with hostility. Efforts are constantly made to intrust the discharge of these new functions to the officials of an existing branch of government. When we survey, for example, the extraordinary variety of responsibilities and duties sheltered under the canopy of departments such as the Departments of Interior or of Commerce, it is impossible to conceive of much in the way of an over-all directional effort deriving from the titular heads. What does derive is too frequently atmosphere, not policy, and atmosphere that may bend unduly the shaping of policies by those who have a first-hand acquaintance with the facts. Organization under the formal aegis of a "Secretary" may frequently be a matter of lines drawn upon a departmental blueprint rather than an evolved plan which has as its basis the active and continuing supervision of one superior. It is not without reason that a nation which believes profoundly in the efficacy of the profit motive is at the same time doubtful as to the eugenic possibilities of breeding supermen to direct the inordinately complex affairs of the larger branches of private industry. Yet that nation seems nevertheless willing to organize its government within a pattern which demands such individuals.

The administrative process points to one solution of this paradox. The demand for expertness, for a

continuity of concern, naturally leads to the creation of authorities limited in their sphere of action
to the new tasks that government may conclude to
undertake. Indeed, the creation of an administrative
authority has attended the effort to solve almost
every major economic issue of this century. President Wilson in one generation and President Frank-
lin Roosevelt in another, before their respective in-
cumbencies, criticized the multiplication of administrative agencies; yet their terms of office saw the
organization of a number of these instrumentalities,
for their creation was an inevitable consequence of
the far-reaching measures that were sponsored. The
translation of such legislation into reality called for
technical skill and required the delegation of grave
matters. To resort under these circumstances to the
device of a compact and select personnel for the discharge of these responsibilities was natural and inevitable.

The consequence of leaving new provinces of governmental activity in the hands of existing agencies
has not been too fortunate. The Federal Power Commission remained moribund until its organization as
a committee of three cabinet officials was displaced
by specially chosen commissioners. Despite the fact
that I took a contrary position in 1934, today I am
convinced that securities regulation has had a hap-
pier history through having had its administration
intrusted to a separate commission rather than continuing the Federal Trade Commission as the administrative authority. In point of fact the initial vesting of that jurisdiction with the Federal Trade Commission was accidental. To have accepted the sugges-

tion, originally made to avoid the creation of a new agency, that that Commission should have jurisdiction over the issuance of new securities while supervision over trading in outstanding securities be placed in the hands of the Postmaster General, would have created an utterly incongruous and confusing situation. Though this suggestion never reached the floor of the Congress, a desperate effort was made there to give supervision over these activities to the Federal Trade Commission. By creating a new Commission, however, it was possible to have individuals in charge whose single concern was the problem of securities regulation. They were thus not required to dissipate their energies over a wide periphery by being responsible for the determination of problems of equal public importance but which bore no discernible relationship to securities regulation. The creation of a new Commission also permitted freedom in shaping its internal organization. Overhanging habits and traditions of operation that had been developed as a result of association with a different problem did not mold the new growth. Furthermore, it was not essential to approach the new problems in a way that required their synthesis with preëxisting policies, as would have been the case had such new regulating duties been intrusted to an established body. To illustrate—a measure of advance interpretation of regulatory requirements by opinions given by the legal staff or by specific regulatory action of the Commission was essential in the securities field. Such a policy, however, ran contrary to a very precise tradition which governed the Federal Trade Commission in its operations under the Federal Trade Commission Act for it has consistently refused to elaborate to any degree upon the meaning of that Act. Again, difficulties attended the first registration requirements promulgated by the Federal Trade Commission under the Securities Act of 1933. They arose, in part, from the fact that the experience of the Federal Trade Commission staff with reference to financial requirements had been developed in the field of utilities which, as a security problem under the new Act, constituted only a segment of the much wider area of security enterprise. It was only after there had been a shift in emphasis as well as the acquisition of new expertness, that more appropriate and more penetrating requirements could be developed.

The tendency in the administrative process is, as I have noted, to make for number. And the effect of number is not only that it promotes expertness but, too, it makes for much more effective public responsibility. Such a statement is bound to be challenged by those who draw their concept of administrative management from traditional organizational charts, which, like genealogical trees, stem in symmetrical form from one great original source. But blueprint symmetry is a poor substitute for realism in organization. Placing responsibility directly upon a specific group means that a finger can be publicly pointed at a particular man or men who are charged with the solution of a particular question. This localization of responsibility gives, in turn, to these positions a real attraction for men whose sole urge for public service is the opportunity that it affords for the satisfactions of achievement. If the functions now exercised by the Federal Reserve Board were to be scattered throughout the Treasury Department, the several posts would lose much of their present appeal. But also, responsibility for the solution of the issues now intrusted to that Board would, at least in the public mind, cease to be susceptible of being specifically affixed to any one person or group. In this respect a sharp contrast can be drawn between the administration of the stock exchanges and those exchanges dealing in commodities. Theoretically, the latter are administered by the Secretary of Agriculture under a bureau chief. The effect, without considering in any manner the efficiency of that administration, is that the public, except in rare cases, becomes unable to attach responsibility directly to a given subordinate official. It is equally impossible to affix a like responsibility to the Secretary of Agriculture in view of the almost limitless range of his other duties. Conversely, despite the mistakes that may have occurred in the administration of the National Industrial Recovery Act, it was possible to attach blame or praise, for the policies pursued, directly to the Administrator. On the other hand, where the administration of one phase of that Act—in the petroleum industry—was turned over to the Secretary of the Interior, the sharp pointing of responsibility was dulled, for administration had become virtually anonymous amid the other heterogeneous duties of the departmental head.

Number, of course, is of great importance in a consideration of the total load of responsibilities assumed by government. Indeed, in view of the scarcity of trained personnel and the tendency to demand and make promises far above any practical possibility of realization, the continued assumption of responsibilities may well exceed the limits of governmental action for a given time and place. But assuming a conceded area of governmental action, the existence of a number of specialized administrative agencies need not disturb us. Instead, if appropriate coördination of their policies can be effected, number affords assurance of expertness in the performance of duties and results in a desirable focusing of responsibility.

I have mentioned a broad distinction which underlies types of administrative agencies now in existence. That distinction relates to the difference between those administrative bodies whose essential concern is the economic functioning of the particular industry and those which have an extended police function of a particular nature. Although it is dangerous to deal in motives, yet the reasons which prompted a resort to the administrative process in the latter area would seem to be reasonably clear. In large measure these reasons sprang from a distrust of the ability of the judicial process to make the necessary adjustments in the development of both law and regulatory methods as they related to particular industrial problems.

Admittedly, the judicial process suffers from several basic and more or less unchangeable characteristics. One of these is its inability to maintain a long-time, uninterrupted interest in a relatively narrow and carefully defined area of economic and social activity. As Ulpian remarked, the science of law embraces the knowledge of things human and divine.[15]

15. Dig. 1.1.10.

A general jurisdiction leaves the resolution of an infinite variety of matters within the hands of courts. In the disposition of these claims judges are uninhibited in their discretion except for legislative rules of guidance or such other rules as they themselves may distill out of that vast reserve of materials that we call the common law. This breadth of jurisdiction and freedom of disposition tends somewhat to make judges jacks-of-all-trades and masters of none.

Modern jurisprudence with its pragmatic approach is only too conscious of this problem. To its solution it brings little more than a method of analysis, a method that calls upon the other sciences to provide the norms. It thus expands rather than contracts areas of inquiry. If the issues for decision are sociological in nature, the answers must be on that plane. If the problem is a business problem, the answer must be derived from that source. But incredible areas of fact may be involved in the disposition of a business problem that calls not only for legal intelligence but also for wisdom in the ways of industrial operation. This difficulty is intrinsic to the judicial process. It is enhanced under our constitutional system which permits judges to disregard those solutions reached by other governmental agencies, such as the legislative and the administrative, when the solution appears to them unfair, unreasonable, or unwise.[16]

16. "The appeal to the courts against something complained of as arbitrary or unreasonable is usually based on the hope that some court will find it inexpedient—in the high sense of answering no necessity of the civilized requirements of the day. . . . That method of decision makes every case one of fact, and yet under our system produces as precedents the opinions on those facts of

The tendency to encourage specialization in the judicial process is of long standing. Indeed, the courts of King's Bench, Exchequer Chamber, and Common Pleas, originally had this impulse underlying their organization, and for a time developed different doctrinal approaches to the same problems.[17] Later we find admiralty, probate, and divorce intrusted practically to specialized hands. In this country the exclusive grant of jurisdiction in admiralty to the federal courts sprang, in part, from that same desire. As matters have developed, probate is generally specialized in state courts in the *nisi prius* stages and practical specialization occurs frequently in the field of criminal law. The federal judiciary has developed a peculiar competence in bankruptcy, receivership, patents, trade-marks, and copyrights, in addition to admiralty. In tax law the Board of Tax Appeals is a specialized tribunal; in tariff and patent law the Court of Customs and Patent Appeals has special competence; and, with the exception of the minor claims that can be prosecuted in the District Courts under the Tucker Act, the Court of Claims deals exclusively with claims of a contractual character arising out of governmental activity.

In the field of unfair competition and monopoly, and in the field of labor, there was widespread dis-

a jury of judges, who in all good conscience are necessarily actuated or dominated by mental attitudes or predilections based on heredity, environment, and education, as all other juries are. This is truly a most unsatisfactory result from a juridical standpoint." Hough, *Covert Legislation and the Constitution* (1917) 30 Harv. L.Rev. 801, 810.

17. See Holdsworth, *History of English Law* (5th ed., 1931), Vol. I, chap. III.

trust of the courts' ability to evolve workable concepts to direct the economic forces which had posed these problems. Some of this distrust found its source in the belief that the resolution of these matters required a condition of uninterrupted supervisory interest that was incompatible with the demands of judicial office. Then, too, it seemed desirable to have some uniformity in approach, a uniformity that under the judicial process could only be attained by the time-consuming and expensive device of appeals to the court of last resort.

To these considerations must be added two others. The first is the recognition that there are certain fields where the making of law springs less from generalizations and principles drawn from the majestic authority of textbooks and cases, than from a "practical" judgment which is based upon all the available considerations and which has in mind the most desirable and pragmatic method of solving that particular problem. In the period preceding the World War commentators upon decisions relating to these problems frequently pointed to the fact that such judgments were determined much less by accepted "legal principles" than by given political, economic, and social considerations—a pedantic way of expressing the term "practical." Then, once having been convinced of the validity of this analysis, these juristic writers thereupon crossed the Rubicon of legal tradition to declare openly that judges made rather than discovered the law. This view was particularly vocal in the fields of monopoly and labor. Here distrust based itself upon the belief that the men who composed our judiciary too often held economic and social opinions opposed to the ideals of their time. The distrust was not without foundation. In the field of monopoly judges had so erased and altered the blank check that had been given to them by the Sherman Act as to afford considerable doubt whether it was not now best to tear the instrument to pieces rather than attempt to decipher its value. In labor law, the course of decision by the Supreme Court of the United States aroused such hostility that in 1930 a nominee to that Court met defeat in the Senate primarily because he was true to the Court's doctrines.[18]

The second consideration is, perhaps, even more important. It is the fact that the common-law system left too much in the way of the enforcement of claims and interests to private initiative. Jhering's analysis of the "struggle for law"—the famous essay in which he indicated that the process of carving out new rights had resulted from the willingness of individuals as litigants or as criminal defendants to become martyrs to their convictions[19]—pointed only to a slow and costly method of making law. To hope for an adequate handling of the problem of allowable trade practices by the sudden emergence of a host of Pyms and Hampdens was too delightfully visionary to be of much practical value. The retaliatory powers of business associates or competitors is today such

18. See "Extracts from the Proceedings Relative to the Rejection by the United States Senate of the Nomination of Judge John J. Parker as Associate Justice of the Supreme Court of the United States," Landis, *Labor Law* (1934), p. 141.
19. Jhering, *The Struggle for Law* (Lalor's trans., 1879).

an immensely powerful force that few persons care to run the risk of its offensive vengeance in the effort to secure what they might deem to be their legal rights. Indeed, one of the first measures adopted by the Federal Trade Commission, and pursued by every agency that has a similar problem, was to keep secret the names of such persons as might choose to complain to it of an unfair business practice.[20]

True, the criminal law offered a partial solution of the difficulty, but an insufficient one. A criminal action changes the entire atmosphere of litigation. The traditions of the common law in criminal cases erect new and imposing barriers to prosecution. Juries are always an uncertain factor, while a judge, in his charge, may exhibit such disrespect for the policy of the law as to make acquittal almost certain. Moreover, prosecuting agencies, like courts, have difficulty in developing that single-mindedness of devotion to a specific problem. Without such devotion their power and efficiency may be effective in particular cases but it would fall substantially short of promoting an enlightened long-term development of law and administration in a particular field.

The demand for a power to initiate action was one of the primary purposes underlying the creation of the Federal Trade Commission.[21] The device thus evolved has since been adopted by many administrative agencies, among them the Securities and Exchange Commission and the National Labor Relations Board. Its uses and abuses already form one of

20. 1916 ANN. REP. F.T.C. 7.

21. See Henderson, *The Federal Trade Commission* (1924), p. 26.

the most interesting chapters of the administrative process. This we shall later have to explore. It is sufficient at this juncture to note that despite criticism the tendency to employ that administrative technique has been on the increase.

The power to initiate action exists because it fulfils a long-felt need in our law. To restrict governmental intervention, in the determination of claims, to the position of an umpire deciding the merits upon the basis of the record as established by the parties, presumes the existence of an equality in the way of the respective power of the litigants to get at the facts. Some recognition of the absence of such equality is to be found in rules shifting the burden of proof and establishing *prima facie* and even conclusive presumptions of fact or of law. In some spheres the absence of equal economic power generally is so prevalent that the umpire theory of administering law is almost certain to fail. Here government tends to offer its aid to a claimant, not so much because of the grave social import of the particular injury, but because the atmosphere and conditions created by an accumulation of such unredressed claims is of itself a serious social threat.

Characteristic illustrations of this situation are not only the problems of unfair trade competition or unfair labor practices but equally problems of the relationship between investor and management. The classic theory of corporate reorganization conceives of a proposed plan of reorganization as a tentative bargain between various classes of creditors and stockholders and the confirmation of that plan after the requisite majority of assents have been given by the corporate constituency. Viewed as an adaptation of democratic processes the theory has much to commend it. As a practical matter, however, the smaller creditor or stockholder is normally helpless in the face of a plan that has the sponsorship of the management, the bankers, and a few of the larger security-holders. To the smaller security-holder the cost of making an investigation of the kind necessary to demonstrate either that there has been no fair disclosure of the implications of the plan to the corporate constituency, or that it is so inequitable as not to justify confirmation, is so excessive that his wisest course, generally, is to sell out at the best figure he can obtain by badgering and threatening management.[22] The practical ineffectiveness of the common-law remedy is leading to the device of requiring an independent administrative examination of the merits both of the plan and the methods of soliciting assents to the plan.[23] The exercise of these powers extends far beyond earlier concepts of fraud or deception to require the "independent" exploration of claims and some assurance of loyalty by those who represent the bargainors.[24]

One other significant distinction between the administrative and the judicial processes is the power of "independent" investigation possessed by the for-

22. See S.E.C., *Report on the Study and Investigation of the Work, Activities, Personnel and Functions of Protective and Reorganization Committees* (1937), Part I, Sec. III.

23. See Dodd, *The Securities and Exchange Commission's Reform Program for Bankruptcy Reorganizations* (1938) 38 CoL.L. Rev. 223, 225–245.

24. See In the Matter of International Paper and Power Co., S.E.C. Holding Company Act Releases Nos. 641, 642, 770 (1937).

mer. The test of the judicial process, traditionally, is not the fair disposition of the controversy; it is the fair disposition of the controversy *upon the record as made by the parties.* True, there are collateral sources of information which often affect judicial determinations. There is the more or less limited discretion under the doctrine of judicial notice; and there is the inarticulated but nonetheless substantial power to choose between competing premises based upon off-the-record considerations. But, in strictness, the judge must not know of the events of the controversy except as these may have been presented to him, in due form, by the parties. Although the power to summon witnesses upon his own initiative in certain cases may theoretically be possessed by him, yet as a matter of fact it is not exercised. The very organization of his office prevents him from doing so. Except in a few cases where the costs of such an investigation can be charged against the *res* that is the subject matter of the litigation, no funds are available for the purpose; no subordinates are at his beck and call competent to perform the function. Nor is he permitted to conduct an investigation to determine what policy is best adapted to the demands of time and place, even though he is aware that sooner or later he will be confronted with the necessity, through the processes of judicial decision, of shaping policy in that particular field. Nor is it, traditionally at least, part of his judicial office to bring to the attention of other departments of government the shortcomings of the law that he feels himself bound to apply.

On the other hand, these characteristics, conspicuously absent from the judicial process, do attend the administrative process. For that process to be successful in a particular field, it is imperative that controversies be decided as "rightly" as possible, independently of the formal record the parties themselves produce. The ultimate test of the administrative is the policy that it formulates; not the fairness as between the parties of the disposition of a controversy on a record of their own making. In securities regulation, for example, the two problems of the admission of securities to unlisted trading and the striking of securities both from listed and unlisted trading, are pertinently significant.[25] Here it soon became obvious that to determine these matters purely upon

25. See Securities Exchange Act, §§ 12(d), 12(f). As illustrative of the procedure on the striking of securities from listed trading, see In the Matter of Conn. Ry. & Lighting Co., Securities Exchange Act Release No. 1032 (1937); In the Matter of Allen Industries, *id.*, No. 1027 (1937); In the Matter of Richfield Oil Corporation, *id.*, No. 1549 (1938). As illustrative of the procedure of striking securities from unlisted trading, see In the Matter of Am. District Tel. Co. (New Jersey) 7% Conv. Cum. Pfd. Stock, *id.*, No. 1283 (1937); In the Matter of City and Suburban Homes Co., *id.*, No. 1012 (1937); In the Matter of Security-First Nat'l Bk. of Los Angeles, 1 S.E.C. 923 (1936); In the Matter of Piedmont & Northern Ry. Co., 1 S.E.C. 916 (1936). As illustrative of the procedure in admitting securities to unlisted trading, see In the Matter of Applications by the N.Y. Curb Exchange, *etc.*, Securities Exchange Act Release No. 1541 (1938); In the Matter of Applications of the San Francisco Curb Exchange, etc., *id.*, No. 1528 (1938); In the Matter of Applications by the N.Y. Curb Exchange, etc., *id.*, No. 1377 (1937); In the Matter of Applications by the Boston Stock Exchange, etc., *id.*, No. 1298 (1937); In the Matter of Applications by the San Francisco Curb Exchange, etc., *id.*, No. 1339 (1937); In the Matter of Applications by the Philadelphia Stock Exchange, etc., *id.*, No. 1312 (1937); In the Matter of Applications by the Pittsburgh Stock Exchange, etc., *id.*, No. 1139 (1937).

the record as the parties made it, would lead to results governed more by chance than by the application of a consistent policy. The Commission itself is theoretically not a party to the disposition of these proceedings. Ordinarily the contest as it arises poses an issue between management and an exchange, or a trading interest, as advanced by a dealer or broker in the over-the-counter market. The Commission's staff, however, has usually assumed the burden of exploring the facts and of counseling the parties with reference to the nature of the issues that may be involved. Similarly, the burden of presenting the facts in unfair competition cases rests with the Federal Trade Commission; to have left it with the consumer or even a competitor would, in the normal situation, have amounted to a denial of justice.

Illustrative of the policy of persistent exploration is the practice of the Federal Trade Commission in the disposition of cases arising under Section 7 of the Clayton Act. While the effectiveness of this provision has been practically destroyed by the decisions of the Supreme Court of the United States,[26] nonetheless, as a routine matter, the Commission, upon its own initiative, still investigates every acquisition by one company of the securities of another, where such a transaction may be thought to involve, in any way, a question under that Section. The presentation of these and other cases by one body, rather than by a heterogeneous group of individual claimants or even

26. F.T.C. v. Western Meat Co., 272 U.S. 554 (1926); International Shoe Co. v. F.T.C., 280 U.S. 291 (1930); Arrow-Hart & Hegeman Electric Co. v. F.T.C., 291 U.S. 587 (1934). Cf. In the Matter of Vanadium-Alloys Steel Co., 18 F.T.C. 194 (1934).

by district attorneys with varying sympathies and abilities, permits the development of consistency in approach to such problems, as well as the creation of effective routines of investigation and examination. The deep significance of these factors has been aptly phrased by Gerard Henderson in his observation that ". . . the science of administration owes its being to the fact that most government affairs are run by men of average capabilities, and that it is necessary to supply such men with a routine and a ready-made technique. . . ."[27]

Equally deserving of notice is the power that the administrative possesses to conduct independent explorations as a prelude either to the fashioning of policies, by way of case decision and specific regulations, or to the obtaining of additional powers from the legislature in order to achieve more effective control over an industry. Of the latter little need be said. Such investigations as that of the utility problem undertaken by the Federal Trade Commission, or the one in the field of corporate reorganization conducted by the Securities and Exchange Commission, are fresh in the public mind. Both threw an illuminating light on those fields, and results that count are attributable, directly and indirectly, to their findings. The operation of the other type of exploration, however, is less commonly known. It may consist of a series of conferences preceding the promulgation of regulations. That was the character, for example, of the investigation pursued by the Securities and Exchange Commission preliminary to the adoption of

27. Henderson, *The Federal Trade Commission* (1924), p. 328.

its accounting regulations; and these rules, as one of the leading accountants of this country observed, did more in one month to advance the science of accounting than had been accomplished by years of futile committee work within the professional societies.[28] This particular research obtained the coöperation of the country's leading accountants, the comptrollers of the greater corporations whose securities were listed on the exchanges, and professors and teachers concerned with the advancement of accounting knowledge and method.

One further illustration of the same technique will, perhaps, give more point to the observation. This relates to the experience of the Securities and Exchange Commission in dealing with the filing by corporations of so-called confidential information. The Securities Exchange Act empowered the Commission to determine that certain information did not need to be disclosed if the Commission was convinced that such disclosure would do more harm than good.[29] That corporations were reluctant to disclose certain matters was manifested by hundreds of requests for confidential treatment of information dealing with the salaries of management and the cost of goods sold. The latter, particularly, was considered by these corporations as a matter whose concealment was of vital necessity. Disclosure, it was claimed, meant injury to the business because it would enable competitors to gauge more accurately the existing margin of profit and thus have the information with which to adopt a price-cutting policy. It was sub-

---

28. See Eric L. Kohler in (1935) 10 ACCOUNTING REV. 102.
29. Securities Exchange Act, § 24.

mitted, further, that disclosure of costs would encourage and permit large customers to use their buying power as a leverage to reduce prices to a point which, in their judgment, gave the selling corporation its "appropriate" ratio of profit. These claims, on their face, seemed to have considerable merit. Moreover, the protestations of the claimants' representatives were normally so importunate as to create the belief that the claim had content. On the other hand, while their number was small, a select few of the investment statistical services were of the opinion that information on gross sales and cost of goods sold was indispensable for an intelligent appreciation of the financial performance of a company.[30]

These were the considerations as the record was built up without exhaustive, independent inquiry, and on the basis of that record, the claim, when made, was quite generally allowed. Some doubts remained, however, as to the general merits of these claims, and because of them a special investigation of the problem was initiated. That investigation, to put it concretely, involved the time of three lawyers and aid from analysts and accountants. It carried them over almost all of the country east of the Mississippi. Upon the basis of their research several facts, of great consequence in relation to the disposition of these claims, were discovered. One was that the figures had little to do with the motivating force which determined buying policies or price competition. Of

---

30. See Morrison, *Reports to Stockholders* (1935) 10 ACCOUNTING REV. 77. Contrast the attitude of leaders of the accounting profession as expressed in a memorandum printed in the BULLETIN OF THE AMERICAN INSTITUTE OF ACCOUNTANTS, Feb. 15, 1935.

equal importance was the discovery that the figures were very rarely a real secret. Often they were common knowledge in the industry; and very frequently they had already been publicly filed, without a murmur of protest, in various state capitals, in response to the requirements of local tax legislation. Decisional policy, naturally, and rightly, shifted after the results of the investigation were received.[31] In case after case, as intimations of that shift in policy were brought home to corporations thus affected, requests for confidential treatment of these figures were withdrawn, and what can most appropriately be described as a rout took place.[32] Instances, of

31. See, *e.g.,* the amendment of Form A-1 to eliminate the authorization to omit information relating to gross sales and cost of goods sold upon a statement by the registrant that its business would be injured by disclosure, and also the amendment of Form A-2 to eliminate the authorization to omit this information where corresponding information filed under the Securities Exchange Act had been granted confidential treatment. Securities Act Releases Nos. 1291, 1292 (1937).

32. On April 13, 1937, the Securities and Exchange Commission announced that the American Tobacco Company, P. Lorillard Company, R. J. Reynolds Tobacco Company, and the United States Tobacco Company had withdrawn their appeals in various United States Circuit Courts of Appeals from the action of the Commission denying confidential treatment to information which they had filed relating to gross sales and cost of goods sold. On the same day the Commission denied the request of the Liggett & Myers Tobacco Company for confidential treatment of this information. Securities Exchange Act Release No. 1140. Two days later the Commission announced that the American Can Company and the National Biscuit Company had withdrawn their appeals in the United States Circuit Court of Appeals from the action of the Commission denying confidential treatment of gross sales and cost of goods sold and that the General Foods Corporation had withdrawn its application for confidential treatment of this information. *Id.,* No. 1146. On April 17, 1937, the Commission announced

course, occurred where the claim had merit and cases even now are pending where there is present a deep-seated and genuine disagreement as to the desirability of disclosure.

I have dwelt at some length upon this problem for it illustrates neatly the employment of a technique which could not possibly have characterized the judicial process. In this particular field of investment analysis and industrial policy, the expertness that was essential for an intelligent disposition of these problems was lacking at the outset even in the administrative. This was only to be expected, for knowledge of these matters was confined to a very limited group of individuals. It had to be discovered and in part created, and initiative to that end had to be furnished by the body charged with disposition. To have relied, simply, upon such considerations as parties claimant before that agency produced, subjected merely to the cross-fire of nonspecialized counsel,

that the Torrington Company had withdrawn its appeal in the United States Circuit Court of Appeals from the action of the Commission denying confidential treatment of the same information. On the same day it was announced that confidential treatment of these items had been denied to the Hamilton Watch Company, the F. E. Myers & Brother Company, and the Valspar Corporation. *Id.*, No. 1150. On April 21, 1937, the Commission announced that it had denied confidential treatment of a similar request of the North American Rayon Corporation. *Id.*, No. 1157. On May 10, 1937, the Commission announced the withdrawal of requests for confidential treatment of this information by the Chrysler Corporation, the Clark Controller Company, the Federal-Mogul Corporation. *Id.*, No. 1190. On June 10, 1937, the Commission announced the denial of confidential treatment of these items in the cases of the Electric Auto-Lite Company, the Diamond Match Company, and the Bower Roller Bearing Company. *Id.*, No. 1241.

would have afforded scant solution; it would have resulted probably in the continuance of the admittedly unhealthy atmosphere of concealment which had thitherto dominated financial reporting.

It is in the light of these broad considerations that the place of the administrative tribunal must be found. The administrative process is, in essence, our generation's answer to the inadequacy of the judicial and the legislative processes. It represents our effort to find an answer to those inadequacies by some other method than merely increasing executive power. If the doctrine of the separation of power implies division, it also implies balance, and balance calls for equality. The creation of administrative power may be the means for the preservation of that balance, so that paradoxically enough, though it may seem in theoretic violation of the doctrine of the separation of power, it may in matter of fact be the means for the preservation of the content of that doctrine.

There is no doubt but that our age must tolerate much more lightly inefficiencies in the art of government. The interdependence of individuals in our civilization magnifies too greatly its cost. The pressure for efficiency has led elsewhere to concentrations of power on a scale that beggars the ambitions of the Stuarts. Our democratic processes have been evolving a different answer and in the form and extent of that answer may lie much of relevance to the matter of their endurance.

II. THE FRAMING OF POLICIES: THE RELATIONSHIP OF THE ADMINISTRATIVE AND LEGISLATIVE

SOMEWHAT hysterically the President's Committee on Administrative Management has referred to the administrative process, as illustrated by the existing independent regulatory commissions, as a "fourth branch" of the government. Its sweeping condemnation of the process seems to proceed almost upon the mystical hypothesis that the number "four" bespeaks evil or waste as contrasted with some beneficence emanating from the number "three." The desirability of four, five, or six "branches" of government would seem to be a problem determinable not in the light of numerology but rather against a background of what we now expect government to do.

This attachment to the number "three" derives from a too casual reading of constitutional history. For constitutional law fails to give any such simple answer. We have already described enough of the rise of the administrative process to illustrate how law and practice have in some measure adjusted themselves to the realities of modern government. We have noted that political development represents a picture of increasing reliance by our society upon the administrative process. The rise of the process has, however, been attended by difficulties; difficulties with the law and difficulties attendant upon the fashioning of these new instruments of power.

The legislative process, the judicial process, and the executive process all imply the idea of delegation from some ultimate source of power. In American democratic theory as in American constitutional law, that source of power is professedly the people of the United States. A grant of power or authority bears with it a privilege to act but only within a given frame of reference. Analysis of the judicial power, the legislative power, and the executive power will expose what limitations are implicit in the grant of such powers as well as what rights are derivable from them. To rehearse the decisions in these fields is unnecessary. It is no secret that they often suffer from that finely spun logomachy which is the delight of lawyers and judges. But overshadowing this innocent and dangerous playing with words is the fact that it is our political history that has given the content that these constitutional concepts possess. For just as the story of judicial power sums up the history of the administration of justice by English and American courts, so legislative power "precipitates centuries of Parliamentary history and decades of colonial practice."[1]

Because our history gives some measure of solidity and form to otherwise loose notions of power, to create a "court" or a "legislature" we need do little more than grant judicial or legislative power, for such a grant will convey authority to an agency to act in accordance with our historically molded ideas of power as they relate to a court or a legislature.

---

1. Landis, *Constitutional Limitations on the Congressional Power of Investigation* (1926) 40 Harv.L.Rev. 153, 156.

Standards to guide the exercise of power by such agencies can be omitted or need only be expressed in the vaguest terms. The subject matter over which they are to exercise jurisdiction can merely be generally indicated. Moreover, the powers necessary to implement these grants of jurisdiction as well as the procedures controlling the manner in which these powers are to be exercised need be set forth only in the very broadest terms.

But the grant of administrative power presents a totally different picture. There has been too little history to give the term "administrative power" a content in any way comparable in impressiveness and historical significance to that conveyed by the expressions "legislative" or "executive power." The boundaries of any grant of administrative power are still a matter of the interpretation of statutes, an interpretation that too infrequently partakes of the character of exposition.[2] The administrative process has often to survive in an atmosphere charged with resentment of its significance and of its force. Its bending of judicial doctrine and procedure to realistic curvatures tends sometimes to offend the courts

2. Compare the interpretation given to the Public Utility Holding Company Act by the Securities and Exchange Commission in In the Matter of the Application of International Paper and Power Co., where the majority of the Commission gave expression to the temper it believed should govern the interpretation of that Act: "To interpret our powers under our fundamental Act with undue strictness at this stage in our growth would be to sacrifice upon the altar of a by-gone legal formalism our ability to perform adequately our allotted task. It would, indeed, be for us to make the mistake which Chief Justice Marshall happily avoided in his exposition of a great organic act in *M'Culloch* v. *Maryland*, 4 Wheat. 316." Holding Company Act Release No. 642.

that supervise its activities. Its relative isolation from the popular democratic processes occasionally arouses the antagonism of legislators who themselves may wish to play a controlling part in some activity subject to its purview.

Constitutional theories as to the delegation of power have thus assumed an important role in the creation and formation of the administrative. In 1916 Elihu Root voiced the opinion that, due to the inexorable growth of administrative agencies, "the old doctrine prohibiting the delegation of legislative power has virtually retired from the field and given up the fight."[3] But in two decisions in 1935, the Supreme Court of the United States had occasion to invoke that doctrine when it overthrew powers granted to presidential authorities to deal with one aspect of the petroleum problem and to carry out the provisions of the National Industrial Recovery Act.[4] With the niceties of the doctrine there set forth—when it becomes, as one justice has described it, "a roving commission," and when it is merely "canalized within banks that keep it from overflowing"[5]—I shall not concern myself. For good or ill these distinctions are more than literature; they are now law.

A principle that runs through the many decisions on delegation of power, however, is that the grant of the power to adjudicate must be bound to a stated objective toward which the determination of claims

3. Root, *Addresses on Citizenship and Government* (1916), p. 534.

4. Panama Refining Co. v. Ryan, 293 U.S. 388 (1935); Schechter Poultry Corp. v. United States, 295 U.S. 495 (1935).

5. See Mr. Justice Cardozo dissenting in Panama Refining Co. v. Ryan, *supra,* 435, 440.

must tend, and, further, that the grant of the power to regulate must specify not only the subject matter of regulation but also the end which regulation seeks to attain. Manifestly, the precision with which these objectives are expressed will vary with each piece of legislation because of the literary qualifications of the particular draftsman as well as the susceptibility of the subject matter to precise delineation. Moreover, it should be remembered that the objectives which frequently characterize political action may not be too discernible. Legislation by the democratic method has this tendency. Wise and honest public men may become jointly interested in the need for altering the trend in a particular industry. They will agree that, basically, the public interest ought to be the governing factor in that industry's future activities, but, for various reasons, they will hold conflicting opinions as to how that public interest can best be served. Legislation, which thus is forced to represent compromise, does so by the use of vague phraseology. Or that phraseology may result not so much from political compromise but from conviction that its vagueness expresses, accurately enough, the existing lack of exact knowledge of the subject.

It is difficult to assess the importance of insisting upon definitive standards. The area of their appropriate use is certainly not deducible from a reading of the judicial literature dealing with constitutional limitations upon the right to delegate power. Unhappily, this tends to become dogmatic, emphasizing too much the language of delegation rather than its purpose. It casts doubt upon the validity of certain ways of delegating power more because of the manner of expression than because of the scope of power. Many administrators who have had to struggle with the problem of translating a statutory scheme of regulation into a working reality would have welcomed, at least in a limited form, the power conferred by the so-called Henry VIII clauses in English legislation. These celebrated clauses give the administrative power to modify the provisions of legislation insofar as it may appear to be necessary to bring the scheme of regulation into effective operation.[6] A grant of this nature, limited in time, might prove serviceable as well as immune from abuse. But under existing decisions in the United States it would clearly seem to come within the judicially condemned category of "roving commissions."

Nor has political science developed the answer to the need for an administratively realistic as well as judicially acceptable formula. Indeed, it is doubtful as to whether it ever can. For that very reason, it becomes important to examine the subject from a different standpoint—to view it not in terms of synthesizing the dicta of judicial opinions but rather of considering the appropriate area of administrative discretion. The distinctions in the scope of administrative power as they come to the surface in legislation at this period of our development derive little from theory. Rather the facts upon which the legislation operates determine the given areas of discretion. Great differences, for example, will be found to exist between the discretionary authority given to the administrative under the Securities Act of 1933

6. For a discussion of the use of these clauses, see *Report of Committee on Ministers' Powers* (1932), Cmd. 4060, 36, 65.

and the Securities Exchange Act of 1934. Broad
powers to exempt securities from the operation of
the 1934 Act were granted to the Commission.[7] They
have been widely employed in the process of adjust-
ing, by progressive stages, the operation of the Act
to the various classes of securities traded upon exchanges that require different, almost individual,
treatment.[8] No like power was given the Federal
Trade Commission or its successor to exempt classes
of securities, even for a time, from the operation of
the registration provisions of the Securities Act of
1933; and this despite the fact that the classes of
securities embraced by that Act were more numerous
and more varied. The data required of registering
corporations under the 1934 Act were only briefly
indicated and even the disclosure of these was not
mandatory.[9] On the other hand, under the 1933 Act

7. Securities Exchange Act, § 3(12).
8. See, *e.g.*, the exemption of all securities for a period of readjustment by regulation of Sept. 28, 1934, Securities Exchange
Act Release No. 13; the exemption of temporarily registered securities from the requirements of Section 12, and of securities admitted
to unlisted trading from Sections 12, 13, and 16, *id.*, 83, 123 (1935);
the exemption of securities, the income of which is guaranteed by
states or political subdivisions thereof, *id.*, 279 (1935); the exemption of all securities for a fortnightly period of readjustment, *id.*,
289 (1935); the exemption of foreign governmental securities, foreign corporation securities, American deposit certificates, pending
the adoption of appropriate forms for registration, *id.*, 290
(1935); the exemption of securities of issues in bankruptcy or receivership or in process of reorganization under Sections 77 or
77(b) of the Bankruptcy Act, pending the adoption of appropriate forms, *id.*, 291 (1935). Contrariwise, under the Securities Act,
although no forms were ready sufficiently prior to its effective
date, the Federal Trade Commission was nevertheless compelled to
require registration. Securities Act Release No. 4 (1933).
9. Securities Exchange Act, § 12.

the requirements were extensive and the power of the
administrative to detract from the statutory demands
was severely limited.[10]

These differences did not derive from political
theory. The presence of a very limited discretionary
power in the administrative to depart from the positive requirements of the 1933 Act arose from the
partial distrust, held by the Congress, as to the
quality and courage of the administrative. There was
then a prevailing lack of confidence in the member-
ship of the Federal Trade Commission.[11] A deliberate
effort, therefore, was made, in the 1933 legislation,
to define the duties and activities of the administrative in such a detailed manner as to make administration almost a matter of mechanical and compulsory
routine. By the time the 1934 Act was passed the
situation had changed. Confidence in the ability of
the Federal Trade Commission had returned[12] and
that confidence, in turn, was reflected in the attitude
of the Congress toward the new administrative
authority, leading to the grant of broader discretionary powers. Then, too, the technical difficulties incident to securities regulation had come to be appre-

10. Securities Act, § 7, Schedules A, B.

11. See, *e.g.*, the opposition in the Senate to the confirmation of
Commissioner William E. Humphrey, 75 CONG.REC. 2790–2792
(1932); the effort of the House to cut the annual appropriations
to the Commission, 76 CONG.REC. 3195–3205 (1933). Even those in
favor of the functioning of the Commission, such as Messrs. La-
Guardia, Cochran, and Amlie, bitterly attacked its present personnel.

12. See, *e.g.*, the opposition in the House to the Bulwinkle
amendment that sought to shift the administration of the Securities Exchange Act from the Federal Trade Commission to a new
commission, 78 CONG.REC. 8104–8111 (1934).
ment Administration Act.

ciated in much greater degree than theretofore and it was consequently recognized that flexible methods of handling the subject matter were most desirable if regulation was to be thoroughly effective.

Generalization as to the allowable limits of administrative discretion is dangerous, for the field is peculiarly one where differences in degree become differences of substance. It is possible to say, on the one hand, that the responsibility for fashioning a policy, not only of great economic importance but also one that has divided the faiths and loyalties of classes of people, cannot appropriately be intrusted to the administrative; on the other, that the scope of administrative power should not be so narrowly defined as to take away from the administrative its capacity to achieve effectively the purposes of its creation. Such corollaries, however, are meaningless in the abstract. It is problems alone that can give them content, but the content that they should possess must have reference to situations seen in the light of the weaknesses and strength of administrative responsibility.

The problem can be illustrated from an incident that occurred during the passage of the Public Utility Holding Company Act of 1935. As passed by the Senate, the bill called for the abolition of all holding companies, save in those few instances where the continuance of a holding company, in the first degree, was required by provisions of state or foreign law in order to maintain a device for continuing the unified management of an existing integrated public utility system.[13] On the other hand, as passed by the

13. Section 11 in the form in which it passed the Senate can be found in 79 Cong.Rec. 10306 (1935).

House, the bill required the Commission to take such action as would have the effect of confining each holding company organization, in its operations, to a single integrated system. But the House bill also authorized the Commission to exempt any holding company from this requirement if such exemption was found to be consistent with the public interest.[14] We have here two radically different approaches. Putting aside any question as to the merits of the so-called "death sentence" of the Senate bill, it did indicate a definite line of action for the Commission to undertake. The House amendment, however, turned over the whole burning issue of the future of the holding company in the public utility field to the Commission itself without any indication of what it should do with it other than that the public interest should be the guide for Commission action. It was obvious at once that, for the Commission, this was an impossible responsibility.[15] It meant nothing less than that the Commission, rather than the Congress, would become the focal point for all the pressures and counter-pressures that had kept the Congress and the press at a white heat for months. Instead of the controversy being concluded, it would have been protracted interminably with the rooms of the Commission the place of debate rather than the halls of the Congress. Some determination as to the place, generally, of the holding company in the public utility

14. Section 11 in the form in which it passed the House can be found in 79 Cong.Rec. 10508 (1935).

15. See, *e.g.,* the letter on this subject by Chairman Kennedy to Senator Wheeler, the letter from Congressman Pettengill to Chairman Kennedy, and the latter's reply, in 79 Cong.Rec. 10838, 11050, 11248 (1935).

field had first to be made by the Congress before the problem was defined sufficiently for an administrative approach.

A similar problem was presented by the National Industrial Recovery Act. Here a grant of power was made to an administrative body the exercise of which required the interpretation of the expression "fair competition," for that phrase pointed to the area within which codes for industrial operation could be made effective.[16] As a legal matter the term had several possible meanings. It would have been possible for the administrative to have interpreted the expression as the antithesis of the phrase "unfair competition." The many Codes of Unfair Competition would then have been confined in their objectives to the proscription of those trade practices that could fairly be considered to be within the ban of Section 5 of the Federal Trade Commission Act. The administrative would, with reference to industry after industry, have expanded by regulation the application of a standard that had already been outlined by the common law and by the decisional activity of the Federal Trade Commission.

There was, however, no strong indication that the Congress intended that the objectives of the National Industrial Recovery Act were to be so limited. The administrative soon conceived that its authority to standardize trade practices permitted it to insist upon such standardization wherever it was convinced that industrial prosperity would flow therefrom. The adoption of the Steel Code in 1933 signified also a further extension of administrative power, for that

16. National Industrial Recovery Act, § 3.

code indicated a belief on the part of the administrative that it could exercise its power to standardize trade practices in return for the willingness of an industry to grant concessions to labor. "Unfair competition" thus ceased to be the equivalent of the type of trade practices banned by the codes of fair competition. Instead the latter included industrial practices condemned merely because they were thought not to promote the general welfare.

Such an interpretation of its grant of power necessarily precipitated the administrative into the region of altering earlier conceptions as to "monopolistic practices" and "practices in restraint of trade." The point of departure now was no longer a consideration of whether practices should be forbidden because they involved elements of deceit or fraud or impinged upon the ability of competitors to reach a market in their own manner. Instead a practice could be sanctioned or disapproved upon a judgment as to whether its pursuit was desirable in the light of its contribution to the prosperity of the dominant units of the industry or its conformance to an economic theory as to the method by which to bring back prosperity.

The power so to standardize trade practices was filled with danger, for to require uniformity in the pursuit of a particular practice, which might be relatively unobjectionable if engaged in singly by one or more units within an industry, immediately gave to that practice a monopolistic quality. The task of essaying definitions of "monopoly" and "restraint of trade" had already been assigned to two other governmental agencies. Confusion naturally followed. In steel[17] and paper,[18] to mention only two instances, contradictions arose. For here obedience to the promulgated codes would have resulted in violations of outstanding orders issued by the Federal Trade Commission, while obedience to these latter orders would have subjected these companies to criminal penalties for infractions of the codes.

This aspect of the administration of the National Industrial Recovery Act demonstrates the "want of clear and encysting resolution" on the part of the Congress in its grant of administrative power. It points to the impossibility of delegating to the administrative the responsibility of making policy from the very irresolution of the legislature. It is true, of course, that contracting the size of the group responsible for the decision as to policy gives the advantage of permitting a more intimate analysis of the problem. But it does not dispense with the ultimate necessity of arriving at some conclusion based upon conscious selection among available and competing postulates. When those postulates have so enlisted the loyalties and faiths of classes of people, the choice, to

17. Cf. Sections 3 and 4 of the Code of Fair Competition for the Iron and Steel Industry (1933) with the Pittsburgh Plus Order as set forth in In the Matter of United States Steel Corporation, 8 F.T.C. 1, 59 (1924). "The code therefore in effect declares unfair and unlawful the practice of f.o.b. mill-base pricing which the Commission assumed to be fair competition. But more than this, it requires important steel producers to violate the Commission's order and permits all to ignore it." F.T.C., *Practices of the Steel Industry under the Code,* Sen.Doc. No. 159, 73d Cong., 2d Sess. (1934) 64.

18. Compare the trade practices to be followed in the Code of Fair Competition for the Newsprint Industry (1933), with those condemned by the Federal Trade Commission in F.T.C. v. Pacific States Paper Trade Ass'n., 273 U.S. 52 (1927).

have that finality and moral sanction necessary for enforcement, must, as a practical matter, be made according to a method which resolves it as if it were one of power rather than one of judgment. In these fields the administrative suffers, too, because of its closeness to the political branches of government. Division within the administrative will thus either tend to follow political lines or be believed to follow them, and the latter is almost more destructive of its position than the former.

It must be remembered that whether or not the administrative is organized along independent lines, its dependence upon the other departments of government is very great. The executive and legislative control both the means of supply and the extent of the agency's powers. Supply is the life blood of efficient administration and access to the means of supply is a closely confined process in our government. Day in and day out pertinent relationships have to be borne in mind if the administrative is to be sure that some intervener will not deprive it, during the next fiscal year, of the means to carry out a program of action that may already have been begun or authorized. Proceedings before the Budget Bureau or before Appropriations Committees sometimes bring forth an assumption of authority by these bodies beyond their proper functions. It is not unusual for them to question expenditures, not upon the ground that they are unnecessary to achieve a particular end, but upon the ground that any expenditure to effect that end should not be made because the end, though authorized by the Congress, fails to conform to their own conceptions of the direction that government should take.

Of equal importance is the fact that the administrative is dependent on the legislative and executive for an extension of its existing powers as occasion may demonstrate that need. Moreover, the agency must have friends, friends who can give it substantial political assistance with which to fend off measures aimed at circumventing its program or curbing its powers. For, too frequently, there is political opposition, from an active minority, in resistance to a phase of administrative policy, where such policy is not clearly understood by the mass or where it will fail to get adequate consideration from a Congressional majority due to Congressional preoccupation with other matters. Typical of this was the recurring effort of some representatives of the gold and silver mining states to amend the Securities Act of 1933.[19] Mistaking the outcries of a group of fly-by-night promoters for the voice of an industry, they sought special privileges for the business of mining that would have prevented the Act from applying its corrective measures to many of the notorious practices that for years accompanied promotions in this field. Overvaluation, donated stock surpluses, misleading classifications of ore, the "donation" of accessable stock, sought protection under the claim that the operation of the Act was choking the progress of mining. Only a cautious treatment of the problem halted the precipitation of a Congressional battle on

19. See, *e.g.*, H.R. 8836 by Mr. Scrugham in 73d Cong., 2d Sess., S. 2461 by Senator Borah and H.R. 7166 by Mr. White in 74th Cong., 1st Sess.

this subject where the forces of the moneyed strongholds of the East might have succeeded in making an alignment with the Western mining states.

This dependence of the administrative upon the other departments of government, it may be observed at this point, inevitably develops several qualities which, today, do in fact characterize administration. Of these, the practice of patronage is outstanding. Inasmuch as good will is essential in order to assure uninterrupted means for the effective pursuit of policies, personal antagonisms arising out of a disregard of patronage problems cannot be ignored. On occasion it may even be necessary to cement alliances by a wise use of the power of appointment. That subject, however, has received so much attention for so many years that no more than passing comment is necessary.

One factor that has received little attention from students of government is the need for the administrative to give adequate and effective publicity to its achievements. In the field of policy determination, effective publicizing of the policy and of the reasons that underlie it is essential. Only in this way can policy achieve the active or, at least, the tacit acceptance of the industrial group affected. But while such wide and general disclosure is necessary for policy declarations, frequently, however, in the disposition of complaints before the administrative the same intensive publicizing occurs. Thus, if the prevailing political atmosphere is dominated by the "big stick," the government of the day expects of the administrative not merely heat and vigor but even more a show of heat and vigor. The big stick must be shaken by many hands, legislative, executive, and administrative. Hence the initiation of administrative action may be preceded by all the fanfare that public relations' counsel can muster. Similarly, investigations may be dominated more by a desire for the dramatic touch than by a productive and legitimate curiosity.

These factors are presented not as objects of condemnation but rather as illustrations of the factors that condition administrative action and thus make for dependency. It is with an appreciation of their operation that the desirability of delegating issues of a broad political character to the administrative for determination must be weighed. We are, of course, in a region of activity where lines are thin and tenuous, and so the distinctions that can be made between issues appropriately delegable to the administrative must be distinctions of degree. But differences of degree begin to possess meaning only if the scale of their measurement is notched in terms of realities. As the judicial literature upon the subject assumes meaning only in terms of the applications of the broad principles that are announced, so to make plain my approach I must resort to further illustrations. This time I choose a sample of delegation that in my judgment is within the appropriate sphere of administrative action.

Section 9 of the Securities Exchange Act of 1934 makes it unlawful to engage in a series of transactions for the purchase or sale of securities in order to peg, fix, or stabilize the price of a security in contravention of such regulations as the Securities and Exchange Commission may prescribe as necessary or appropriate in the public interest or for the protec-

tion of investors. In other words, power is granted to
the Commission to deal with pegging as it may deem
best, provided that its judgment flows from a determination to promote the public interest or to protect investors. As a matter of phraseology the grant
is broad, not in terms, to use Mr. Justice Cardozo's
words, "canalized within banks that prevent it from
overflowing." Levees, however, are there to those who
will seek them in the history of the legislation.

Pegging or stabilizing a security was a practice
common in the security world. Its purpose was to
hold the price of a security at or near a certain point
during a period of direct distribution or distribution
by way of rights. If a security, identical with a security already traded on an exchange, was offered to
the public, retail sales at a fixed price could hardly
be successfully pushed if the price on the exchange
should fluctuate. An upward movement might be disastrous in that it could so easily turn downward, and
sales on the exchange effected at prices below the retail offering, obviously would impede the merchandising campaign. These factors thus led the sponsors
to supply such buying power on the exchange as conditions might dictate, and the cost or profit in this
trading account normally would be charged or cred-
ited to the syndicate members in predetermined proportions. The fluctuations on the exchange might, of
course, result from a variety of causes. Among them
is the belief that professional traders, because of the
sponsorship of the issue by important underwriters,
normally act upon the assumption that, in the absence of an unusually adverse market, the price of
the issue for a short time will rise above the offering

price. Thus, it is argued, these men will buy at the offering price and shortly thereafter sell when the hoped-for advance realizes. This, in turn, creates an abnormal selling pressure which will drive the security down to the disadvantage of longer time buyers. Thus a justification is alleged for the underwriters themselves to supply a compensating buying power. Other reasons, which need not here be elaborated, also are claimed to produce abnormal selling pressure in the initial stages of distribution which justify the underwriters in supplying buying power.

This practice of pegging or stabilizing was, however, unquestionably employed for other purposes where it assumed plainly the characteristics of manipulation. Even under those conditions where it may be claimed to be justified, stabilization, it is contended, has economic consequences which, irrespective of the honesty of purpose of the stabilizers, may be fully as serious as those flowing from manipulation. Bad judgment on the original pricing, for example, after the stabilizing activities have been concluded, may bring about as precipitous a decline as may ensue upon the cessation of manipulative activity. These and various other reasons were urged as warranting the complete proscription of such merchandising methods.

This brief and too simple analysis of the stabilization problem does reveal that in its essence the questions it poses concern the extent of permissible merchandising techniques in the security field. Obviously, no reasonable defense could be advanced on behalf of an individual or group of individuals who engaged in exchange transactions for the sole purpose of maintaining a security at a certain level in order thus to have a sounding board for the price at which they were unloading that security upon an uninformed and unsuspecting public. In the light of the legislation itself, that issue is no longer debatable. Stabilization thus becomes relegated to the position of a defensive rather than an offensive tactic— defensive in that its justification must spring from its use to ward off abnormal selling pressures. The extent to which it can be justifiably employed to that end, and the conditions that must surround such employment to insure that its use is restricted to that limited purpose, are not matters that are now my concern. What is important to observe is that the area of the delegated power granted to the Commission is in fact circumscribed by such considerations. That the standards as written into the legislation are broad and vague becomes immaterial; what is significant is that all that remains now to the administrative is the proscription of merchandising techniques to achieve ends which have already been delineated.

I have remarked upon the fact that the standards written into this legislation were broad and vague. They are typical of many similar standards found in modern legislation. Phrases such as "public interest," "protection of investors," "protection of consumers," and others abound in the law. In and of themselves they have, of course, exactly the meaning that we put into them. But as portfolios bearing the form of a thought, they do not reach the administrative in an empty condition. Rather they have already been lined and fitted, so that it becomes impossible for the administrative to pack bricks into what is

ostensibly an overnight bag. For the administrative
the task of grasping the legislative thought should
not be difficult. The meaning of such expressions is,
of course, derivable from the general tenor of the
statute of which they are a part. To read them properly one must catch and feel the pace of the galvanic
current that sweeps through the statute as a whole.
Of significance in this connection is the practice recently adopted in statutory drafting, of reciting the
conditions that lead to and make imperative particular legislation, before setting out the operative provisions of the statute itself. In part this recital takes
the place of the old-fashioned preamble, the passing
of which many men wise in the law have deplored.
Despite the occasional cavalier and cynical treatment of these recitals by the courts, they do help to
create the frame of reference within which the administrative is to operate, and to pose the objective that
was intended to be reached. It is worth remembering
that, at the time of the passage of the Securities Exchange Act of 1934 and the Public Utility Holding
Company Act of 1935, representatives of the exchanges and the utilities were considerably disturbed
at certain of the recitals. As a result they spent no
little effort in an attempt to change some of the language of what professedly is nonoperative phraseology. The years have proven that from their standpoint they were right; for both the trend in meaning
given the operative provisions of the legislation and
the character of subsequent administration was determined, in large measure, by the form and content
of the recitals.

Of the effectiveness of general standards in shaping administration, I can only speak from personal experience and observation. I have little doubt as to their value in guiding the administrative. The technical demands of administration are often so complex and absorbing that their solution tends to shorten vision. Administrative myopia that fails to see the woods because of the abundance of the trees is not uncommon. To take what is thought to be a satisfactory solution of a problem and to set it alongside the statutory grant of power gives a fresh viewpoint, an opportunity to reappraise a result in terms of the broad statutory objective. I have too often seen significant changes take place at this "second reading" stage of administrative action not to have respect for even that broad generality of language.

A marked tendency of modern legislation is to deal with regulatory problems by setting forth less frequently in the legislation itself the particular rules that shall control. More commonly the administrative is given power to prescribe governing regulations in certain spheres of activity. Delegation is thus on the increase. If we contrast, for example, the form of the Interstate Commerce Act with that of the Securities Exchange Act, the difference is immense. Detailed regulative provisions encumber the Interstate Commerce Act. Indeed, that Act has ceased to have the appearance of a constituent document and resembles rather a regulative code. Students of it will recall sympathetically the outcry by Frederick J. Stimson against its cumbrous form, and wish that he had had the opportunity to make good on his boast that the Act could be redrawn "with two days' honest work" to say and effect the same things in four pages.[20] The result of using such a technique is to call over and over again for Congressional amendments. Hardly a Congressional session concludes which has not passed some amendment of a minor or major nature to the Interstate Commerce Act. The Securities Exchange Act presents a very different situation. There, with broad rule-making powers vested in the Commission, amendment becomes necessary only when the administrative is faced with primary problems affecting its powers.

Such delegation of power means, of course, that the operative rules will be found outside the statute book. But it does not follow from this that these rules lack that publicity which, clearly, should attend the imposition of regulatory requirements. Since the establishment of the Federal Register the regulations of administrative agencies are as accessible, if not more so, than the enactments of the Congress. The chief virtue of this modern tendency toward delegation is that it is conducive to flexibility—a prime quality of good administration. The administrative is always in session. Its processes operate with comparative rapidity. By centralization in the drafting of its rules it can preserve the outlines of formal order in its requirements. The agency's compactness gives some assurance against the entry of impertinent considerations into the deliberations relating to a projected solution. I have seen as little as twenty minutes elapse between the drafting and promulgation of a permissive rule where the exigencies of the situation called for quick action. On the other hand, I have watched and participated with the experts for

20. Stimson, *Popular Law-Making* (1910), p. 362.

over two years in a vain attempt to find a solution to a problem which continues to defy even a tentative, experimental answer.

Despite the outcry from time to time by individual members of the Congress against the grant of powers to the administrative to formulate regulatory provisions, on the whole that process today has the respect of the members of the legislative branch of the federal government. Those with experience in legislative matters or with an insight into the difficulties attendant upon bridging the chasm between the phrase "Be it enacted" and law in the sense of controlling human affairs, recognize that it is easier to plot a way through a labyrinth of detail when it is done in the comparative quiet of a conference room than when it is attempted amid the turmoil of a legislative chamber or committee room.

Difficulties in administrative adjustment frequently flow from a too elaborate formulation of standards. Draftsmen or legislators laboring under the impression that the outlines of the problem are relatively clear have sometimes phrased the conditions of administrative action in such detail as to make it difficult effectively to dispose of a pressing situation. Illustrative of this condition was a problem that was conspicuous early in the administration of the Securities Act. One of the subjects covered by the regulatory features of the Act was the matter of foreign governmental issues. The criminal looseness of banking and underwriting practices in the origination and sale of the securities of foreign governments is almost without historic parallel. Particular attention was therefore devoted to devising mechanisms to purify security practices in this field. The point of leverage for the exercise of control was entry into our capital markets. But the march of international events moved more rapidly than the foresight of the Congress. Default on the part of certain foreign governments ceased to be a matter of disgrace at home or a cause of surprise and indignation abroad. Foreign governments soon recognized that their chances of reëntering and tapping our capital markets for additional funds were negligible, at least until another generation should arise which would have forgotten the essential insecurity attached to a bond that had no legal sanction and was now lacking even in moral obligation. The problems that arose no longer concerned efforts to tap our market by the issuance of new securities. The new problems were connected with offers made by defaulting governments to compromise their outstanding obligations. Negotiations might or might not precede these tendered settlements but even these negotiations were likely to be carried on by self-appointed representatives of the creditor classes. The individual creditor was normally helpless in the face of an offer of compromise. No property of the debtor was ordinarily subject to execution; and other legal sanctions were absent. Confronted with this Hobson's choice, it did the individual creditor very little good to learn from an analysis of filed documents that he was being discriminated against in behalf of other creditors, or that the new obligation he was being tendered in exchange for the old had the same practical defects as had characterized the previous contract. Compelling the registration of these offerings, therefore, had only slight value as compared with the utility of requiring registration of a new or a refunding issue. In addition there was almost no leverage for bringing pressure to bear upon the issuing government because the normal leverage—exclusion from our capital markets—was something it did not prize. Yet the statutory requirements called for registration. A danger of insisting upon the assumption of that burden by the issuing government—a burden that called for the revelation of many international skeletons—was that the government might then withdraw the niggardly offer it had decided to make and thereupon leave our nationals with still emptier pockets. Even worse, however, was the fact that to the renewed outcry by debtors against continued default, the foreign government now had the face-saving reply that its efforts to meet its obligations as far as it could had been thwarted by our law.

A situation of this nature obviously was different, in kind, from the normal offering of a foreign governmental issue. The problem was full of domestic and international difficulty. It required careful and gingerly treatment by the administrative in order to retain the principle and the major benefits of disclosure and at the same time to use this power to exact slightly better terms than had originally been proposed. How that was done is another story. The illustration suffices to demonstrate the perils of applying Procrustean standards to a world that breeds both pigmies and giants.

Another example may be found in the Public Utility Holding Company Act of 1935. Supervision over the acquisition by one utility company of the securities of another was, of course, essential in order to prevent the formation of new alliances that would make it more difficult to put into effect the "unscrambling" requirements of Section 11—the so-called death sentence. Consequently the Commission was required to find as a condition to the approval of any such acquisition that the contemplated transaction would "serve the public interest by tending towards the economical and efficient development of an integrated public utility system."[21] In the normal situation that standard is quite appropriate because ordinarily the process takes the form of acquiring a new interest in another utility, or of increasing the existing stock interest in another utility. But shortly after the section went into operation two different types of situations came before the Commission for consideration. One related to the acquisition of new securities in exchange for old securities pursuant to a plan of reorganization of the company whose securities were being acquired. Here the acquiring company substantially had no choice, for in many instances, whether or not it physically acquired the new securities, its old securities by operation of law represented the same interest as that of the new securities. In these cases an order approving an acquisition became a meaningless formality. In other cases the acquiring company might possess the right to refuse to take the new securities and insist upon the purchase of its old

21. Public Utility Holding Company Act, § 10 (c)(2).

securities at an appraised value. But to require it to take this action might result in denying it such recoupment properties as might inhere in the plan of reorganization. In these cases one fact was clear; that such an acquisition, though it might not tend toward integrating the properties of the acquiring company, would not, however, normally increase the difficulty of such "unscrambling" as might thereafter become necessary. Indeed, if the plan of reorganization were successful, the possibilities of subsequent "unscrambling" became enhanced by rendering the securities received by the acquiring company liquid and readily disposable. This practical interpretation of the legislative standard, as a matter of common sense, had to be adopted by the Commission.[22]

A more difficult situation presented itself when the acquiring company was issued rights to purchase further securities in a company in which it already held a common stock interest. The rights might not have a ready market. Even if they did, to require them to be sold would reduce the existing ratio of ownership in the issuing company. To determine the desirability of such a reduction in a piecemeal manner was impractical. On the other hand, exercise of the rights meant only retaining the ratio of ownership in the issuing company which the acquiring company already held, although it did involve increasing the total capital investment of the acquiring company in the issuing company. How to bring this situation under the statutory standard remained a

22. See In the Matter of the Application of the Middle West Corporation, 1 S.E.C. 578 (1936); In the Matter of the Middle West Corporation, 1 S.E.C. 514 (1936).

puzzle, but approvals of such applications, as a practical matter, had to be granted.[23]

Standards, if adequately drafted, afford great protection to administration. By limiting the area of the exercise of discretion they tend to routinize administration and to that degree relieve it from the play of political and economic pressures which otherwise might be harmful. The pressing problem today, however, is to get the administrative to assume the responsibilities that it properly should assume. Political and official life to too great an extent tends to favor routinization. The assumption of responsibility by an agency is always a gamble that may well make more enemies than friends. The easiest course is frequently that of inaction. A legalistic approach that reads a governing statute with the hope of finding limitations upon authority rather than grants of power with which to act decisively is thus common. One of the ablest administrators that it was my good fortune to know, I believe, never read, at least more than casually, the statutes that he translated into reality. He assumed that they gave him power to deal with the broad problems of an industry and, upon that understanding, he sought his own solutions. Limitations upon his powers that counsel brought to his attention, naturally, he respected; but there is an enormous difference between the legalistic form of approach that from the negative vantage of statutory limitations looks to see what it must do,

23. See In the Matter of North Boston Lighting Properties, 1 S.E.C. 260 (1935); In the Matter of Mass. Utilities Associates, 1 S.E.C. 254 (1935); In the Matter of Mass. Lighting Companies, 1 S.E.C. 253 (1935).

and the approach that considers a problem from the standpoint of finding out what it can do.

One difficulty in governmental technique that leads to the narrowing of grants of discretionary power and the resultant nonassumption of responsibility by the administrative is the fact that too little imagination has been employed in considering the manner in which the rule-making power is to be exercised by the administrative. It is possible by a simple device to have the administrative as the technical agent in the initiation of rules of conduct, yet at the same time to have the legislative share in the responsibility for their adoption. Frequently the administrative is faced with the need to exercise a power that lies within the limits of its statutory grant; but the subject matter happens to be of such great public concern that it is desirable to have the more direct democratic processes of our government participate in the decision. An illustration from another field may serve to give point to this problem. Under the statutory authority that had already been granted to him, the President had the power to commit the nation to large expenditures in connection with the Florida Ship Canal. The project, however, partly because of the amount of expenditure that it entailed and partly because it had for various reasons already become the subject of political debate and conflicting allegiance, differed considerably from the regular public works projects to which the President was authorized to allocate public monies. For these reasons it was an act of political wisdom to put back upon the shoulders of the Congress the basic question as to the desirability of allocating the money necessary for the development of this project.[24]

Such tactics, however, are not usually available to the administrative. Besides, they involve a delay that in any case may make their pursuit useless. In English administrative law two techniques have been developed which might be adapted to our needs.[25] Both require proposed regulations to be laid before Parliament. The first provides that a regulation becomes effective within a given period of time, unless prior thereto Parliament shall, by resolution, have disapproved it. The second provides that a regulation shall not become effective until Parliament by resolution approves it. Parliament with reference to this second class of regulations passes them through the mill almost as a matter of routine unless serious objections are made.[26] Such delay as is necessitated by this process is prevented from having any serious effects by giving the administrative authority to make provisional regulations to meet emergencies as they arise.[27]

These techniques have several virtues. For one thing, they bring the legislative into close and constant contact with the administrative. Objections by individual members of the legislature to particular regulatory measures can easily and openly be made. With us, individual legislators who object to particu-

24. See the issue as raised by the Fletcher amendment to the War Department Appropriations Bill, 80 CONG.REC. 3761–3778, 3830–3846 (1936).

25. See *Report of Committee on Ministers' Powers* (1932), Cmd. 4060, 41–42.

26. *Id.,* p. 25.   27. *Id.,* p. 46.

lar administrative regulations, place their objections before the administrative. If the administrative is still opposed and the objectors are insistent, other measures are employed to bring pressure upon the administrative with a view to having it conform to the objectors' wishes. By giving the legislative a definitely recognized share in the exercise of the regulatory power of the administrative, a much more open responsibility of the administrative to the legislature is attained.

Again, the English technique permits the administrative to call upon the legislature to assume some of the responsibility attendant upon action. The legislative thus can help to overcome a hesitancy to take responsibility for action that sometimes makes the administrative process stagnant. With us, however, legislative appraisals of administrative action are infrequently made and when made they come by the less desirable way of Congressional investigation. By that time the regulatory record is cold, tending to lead to criticism of the administrative based upon the hindsight of intervening events. To be effective, the administrative must take the chances of action in the light of what appears wise at the time action is required. The quicker there can be an assessment of a situation as it presently exists, the more accurate will be the appraisal of the quality of administrative handling of such dynamic problems. One difficulty that attends existing methods of evaluating administrative action is that it encourages administrators to "play for the record." Instead of acting with as much foresight as is possible to meet the conditions that are confronted at the time and assuming responsibility in the light of these contemporary facts, the safer course is to rely upon the limitations of governing statutes. In the event that action is taken and subsequently proves wise, the dissentient member's recorded dissent (which is rarely made public at the time) is readily forgotten; but in case the action proves unsuccessful and Congressional investigation follows, that member remains protected by his recorded disapproval.

It would be unwise, of course, to require the adoption of the English techniques in all cases. But when the anticipated administrative action is of large significance, value attaches to their employment. Moreover, it may be well to lodge a discretion in the administrative, giving it the power to depart from its regular procedure of independently adopting regulations, and permitting it to resort to one or another of these devices when, in its discretion, it deems it advisable to have the imprimatur of the Congress upon its action. Members of an administrative agency who might hesitate to take the responsibility of action upon their own initiative might well be willing to take that action subject to such legislative review.

A subsidiary advantage of these techniques is that they would remove many fruitless technical difficulties which have been introduced by the courts in the course of their application to legislative power of the maxim *delegatus non potest delegare*. They afford, too, an ingenious answer to the problem of having a cake and at the same time eating it; for though these devices, virtually, have all the benefits of delegation, they do not run the risk of what the courts have called "abnegation." Should these methods be fully and ap-

propriately employed, we might soon discover that
Elihu Root's prophecy with reference to the retirement of the old doctrine against delegation of power
was approaching some measure of realization.

Another facet of rule-making power that has at-
tracted little attention is the capacity of rules to
clarify the provisions of statutes. Interpretation by
way of adjudication, manifestly, is interpretation
after the event; but the adequate functioning of the
administrative process requires that much interpretation precede the event. It is difficult to generalize
as to the proper scope for the exercise of this *ante
factum* power. Much of the criticism directed toward
the Attorney General's office when the Antitrust
Division assumed the burden of rendering interpretative clearances seems justified. The same method,
essentially, was employed on a wider basis under the
National Industrial Recovery Act. Here, in addition,
a special dispensatory power was presumed to exist.[28]
In its promulgation of the so-called Group II Trade
Practice Conference Rules, the Federal Trade Commission also was giving similar interpretations.[29]
While it is true that justifiable criticism can be leveled
against these exercises of the interpretative power,
that criticism should not lead us to conclude that

28. Two views existed with reference to the meaning of Section
3 of the National Industrial Recovery Act. One regarded the pro-
viso enjoining codes from permitting monopolies or monopolistic
practices as being a limitation upon the power to promulgate
codes. Another, that pursued in practice, regarded the injunction
as merely limiting the President's discretion in ordering the approval of a code.

29. See F.T.C., *Trade Practice Conferences* (1933). Group I
rules set forth what are believed by the Commission to be unfair

there was and is no appropriate area for the issuance of interpretative regulations or advisory opinions.

The clearest case for the exercise of advisory authority is when a transaction receives its legal characteristics from its form. The manner of its performance may determine the extent to which it is within or without the purview of a statute. By the Securities Act of 1933, the Commission was empowered to exempt securities from registration "when the aggregate amount at which such issue is offered to the public" did not exceed $100,000. This line of division between exempt and registerable issues was a purely arbitrary one. Its application in the "normal" instance presented no difficulty. But in the case of the issuance of certificates of deposit or the offering of open-end investment trust certificates, whose daily "offering price" varied with the liquidating price of the securities behind the trust, the application of the statutory rule raised difficulties. The "offering price" of certificates of deposit particularly needed elaboration. Analogical treatment of the problem yielded the ready answer that the "offering price" was the market price of the outstanding securities for which these certificates were being offered in exchange. But since the outstanding securities in fact might have no "market price," there was nothing upon which to base a calculable "offering price." Regulation, there-

methods of competition, illegal within the prohibitions of Section 5 of the Federal Trade Commission Act. Group II rules condemn trade abuses and unethical and wasteful practices. Group I rules are enforced by the Commission like any other violation of law. The role of the Commission in the enforcement of Group II rules is obscure. For criticism of these rules, see Handler, *Unfair Competition* (1936) 21 IOWA L.REV. 175, 253.

fore, became imperative and upon the assumption that these securities ordinarily would be depressed, the Commission took one third of their face value as their value for purposes of calculating the "offering price" of the certificates of deposit offered in exchange for them.[30]

Similarly, under the Securities Exchange Act of 1934, brokers and dealers were required to disclose to customers in writing "at or before the completion of the transaction" whether they were acting as dealers for their own account, as brokers for their customer, or as brokers for any other person. What events completed the transaction "in respect to" a security was a matter that had to be determined in order to have a rule of conduct which could be observed by those engaged in these transactions. Theoretically, three choices were open—the time of making the contract for sale or purchase, the time when the customer parted with value in connection with the transaction, and the time when delivery of the securities was made to or by the customer. For reasons that seemed to carry out the policy of the section and, at the same time, to provide for a simple and workable rule, the Commission chose the second class of events and embodied that choice in an interpretative opinion.[31]

On the other hand, when the legal characteristics of a transaction derive not from its form but rather from a consideration of its substantive effects, advance interpretative action is on dangerous ground.

30. See Form D-1.
31. See Securities Exchange Act Release No. 253 (1935).

It was for this reason that from the very beginning the Commission refused to amplify the statutory term "control"—as it related to a controlling interest or a controlling person—beyond stating the obvious, that "control" was an issue of fact in any given case and that the mere form in which it might be exercised, therefore, was immaterial. Whether a stock interest in fact represented control could not be made to depend upon a mathematical ratio. A 5 per cent ownership of voting stock might in fact be equally as controlling as 51 per cent. This issue of when control exists was believed to be capable of determination in any particular instance by resort to the traditional adversary procedure of litigation, for only in this manner could one be assured of thorough exploration of the relevant facts necessary for judgment. Otherwise interpretation would tend to transform a matter of substance into a matter of form.

It is, of course, no simple matter to find the line of demarcation between subject matters amenable to the interpretative technique. In its anxiety to regularize conduct, the administrative may be lured into rendering interpretative assistance in an inappropriate field, with the result that legitimation tends to derive from the wrong characteristics. The Securities and Exchange Commission made that mistake, in the beginning, by attempting to define "public offerings." It soon realized that advantage was being taken of these definitions. Thereupon it retreated openly from the field and refused to do more than point to the considerations which, it believed, should have primary weight in the course of differentiating the exempt "private offering" from the registerable "public offering."[32]

There are several approaches, varying in their respective worth, that may be employed in exercising interpretative power. The Securities and Exchange Commission has used several. The most authoritative device is the Commission regulation. Another, on a slightly lower level, is the Commission opinion. A third is an opinion by the General Counsel of the Commission. The Commission can repudiate this opinion without getting into the embarrassing position of having openly to repudiate itself. This advantage, however, is more apparent than real, for when the General Counsel's opinion is issued to the public in the form of an official Commission release it has received, prior to its publication, the actual approval of the Commission. A fourth, an informal opinion of the General Counsel, has no such standing. For its quality is stamped upon its face by the concluding phraseology which declares that it represents merely the opinion of the General Counsel and should not be taken as an expression of the views of the Commission. It is commonly employed as a means of responding to inquiries. It receives no publicity nor is it normally a subject of discussion by the Commission as a whole or by any of its individual members. What weight the courts will give these various expressions of administrative judgment and practice remains to be seen. All have developed empirically in response to the needs of administration as those needs were viewed by that particular agency.

This interpretative function of the administrative

32. See Securities Act Release No. 285 (1935).

is not new. It has been exercised from the beginning of the administrative process and, too, has received the approval of the courts. It has been given the tacit endorsement of the legislature.[33] In modern statutes, however, the desirability of exercising such a power has been more openly recognized. The original Securities Act expressly authorized the administrative to define "accounting and trade terms" as they might appear in the Act.[34] To this power the amendments of 1934 added the right to define "technical" terms. Almost any term in such a statute, that had not already received a distinctly legal connotation, would probably have reference to the field of finance and thus might be embraced within the categories represented by the expressions "technical" or "trade" terms. This particular grant of power in the Securities Act is magnified by the addition of a provision which protects bona fide reliance upon any action pursuant to regulations promulgated by the administrative, this notwithstanding the fact that subsequently the judicial power may have concluded that these regulations were beyond the authority delegated to the administrative. This provision has since been copied and seems to have met with general approval.[35]

If interpretative regulatory activity by the ad-

33. Compare the rule of statutory construction giving effect to Congressional acquiescence in the administrative construction of a statute. Patterson v. Louisville & Nashville R. R. Co., 269 U.S. 1, 9 (1925).

34. See Securities Act, § 19(2). For examples of the use of this power, see Securities Act Releases Nos. 47, 96, 184 (1933–34).

35. Section 23(a) of the Securities Exchange Act was amended in 1936 to include such a provision. See Cook, *Certainty in the Construction of the Law* (1935) 21 Am.Bar Ass'n.J. 19.

ministrative is to be criticized, it should be done in the name of omission rather than commission. The fact that at times the administrative may ultimately be compelled to reject its earlier conclusions is no ground for a tradition of inaction. The hesitancy of the Federal Trade Commission to expand its Group I Trade Conference Practice Rules was, in great part, responsible for the forms that the codes of fair competition took under the National Industrial Recovery Act. The Commission might have afforded some answer to the grave questions raised by industry relative to the propriety of certain of its activities under the Sherman and Clayton Acts. Professor Milton Handler of Columbia puts the case for the exercise of this power in language somewhat stronger than I, perhaps, would endorse, but with great emphasis. He says:

The definition of unfair competition by administrative legislation is incomparably superior to definition by administrative decision. The method of judicial exclusion and inclusion does not permit of a sustained, consistent, comprehensive and speedy attack upon the trade practice problem. The case by case determination takes years to cover even a narrow field; it leaves wide lacunae; false starts are difficult to correct and the erroneous decision is just as prolific as a sound ruling in begetting a progeny of subordinate rules. In a controversy between two litigants or between a Commission and a private party, the law making function is distracted by factors which are important to the contestants but irrelevant to the formulation of future policy. The fusion of law and economics, the detailed investigations and hearings, and the precise formulation of rules, all of which are so essential to a proper regulation of competition, are not feasible when law making is but a by-product of the adjustment of controversies. The combination of the two functions may have been justified when knowledge of the workings of competition was sparse and objectives ill-defined. It can no longer be justified today. It would be little short of criminal to rely upon so inefficient a method of law making when more scientific and expeditious devices are available.[36]

The experience under the National Industrial Recovery Act is, perhaps, too fresh in one's mind for such a plea to meet sympathetic understanding. But many other factors intruded into that experiment. The passion for energetic action was too fierce to permit time for the play of disinterested expertness. More than this, one prime difficulty attended the National Recovery Administration and still attends the Federal Trade Commission. That is the enormous expanse of its jurisdiction. Expertness may well be expected to give answers to some of these questions that today still require to be answered, if the area of regulatory operation is limited to the field of possible knowledge. But to assume that any five, ten, or twenty men have the ability to acquire, within their brief official lifetime, the expertness to comprehend the full range of our industrial problems, from aluminum to zinc, is once more to put our trust in supermen. In the business of governing a nation—to paraphrase Gerard Henderson again—we must take into account the fact that government will be operated by men of average talent and average ability and we must therefore devise our administrative processes with that in mind.

In this examination of the relationship, in a few

36. Handler, *Unfair Competition* (1936) 21 Iowa L.Rev. 175, 259.

select areas, of the administrative and legislative, I trust that I have not given the impression that any set formula can be devised to establish with precision the field of action and interaction. My desire has been otherwise. Indeed, my criticism of judicial doctrine dealing with the delegation of power is that it draws too readily upon words, while political theory erects, without those qualifications which responsibility tends to give judges, tripartite doctrines into inviolable forms of political organization. To condemn the administrative process simply because it is a "fourth branch" of government is not to consider what a "branch" implies. Four, five, and six "branches" of government may, of course, coexist without violating Montesquieu's maxim, for the ultimate source and the ultimate division of power remain the same. It is the relationships of the administrative to the three departments of government that are important. The formulation of these relationships must derive from the necessity of attuning the process to the dynamic forces of industrialism as of a particular time and place. Fifteen years ago Cecil Carr in his lectures on *Delegated Legislation* had occasion to point to the variations in the nature of the administrative process in times of war as contrasted with times of peace.[37] But peace, too, has its special requirements. Only as one understands these requirements does it become possible to formulate the appropriate area of administrative action. And wisdom in the formulation of standards, in the grant of powers, is the first step toward realization of those hopes now so definitely held of the administrative process.

37. Carr, *Delegated Legislation* (1921), Preface.

III. SANCTIONS TO ENFORCE POLICIES: THE ORGANIZATION OF THE ADMINISTRATIVE

THE Interstate Commerce Act was passed only fifty years ago—in 1887. During that same year a struggling legal periodical that had just been founded—the *Harvard Law Review*—had this observation to make about what seemed to it an important academic event.

The well-known authority on Railroads, Professor Arthur T. Hadley of Yale, in his recent lecture in Cambridge on the Interstate Commerce bill, expressed himself strongly in favor of leaving the problems of railroad charges and management to work themselves out in the courts as questions arise from time to time. The result of a railroad law thus gradually evolved and perfected to meet the needs of the country would be less injurious to business, and would cause less derangement of economic machinery than any statute or series of statutes, however good.[1]

These comments of Professor Hadley indicate a singular unawareness of the fact that the chief drive for the resort to the administrative process in the field of railroad regulation arose from a recognition that the remedies that the courts could provide were insufficient to make effective the policies that were being demanded.

These implements or remedies to effectuate policies can appropriately be called sanctions. Whereas the

1. (1887) 50 HARV.L.REV. 99.

substance of law, its theories, and its techniques are the subject of continuing instruction and research, sanctions—the means whereby policies can most effectively be translated into reality—have received only casual notice. More than a hundred years ago Jeremy Bentham called attention to a branch of legislation to which he gave the high-sounding name of "transcendental" legislation. He defined it as being the science of "devising a course of legislative acts adapted to prevent offences."[2] He observed that this branch had been more tardily cultivated than any other and he ascribed that to the fact that it demanded "a longer series of observations and meditations more profound." "Nobody," he added, "has undertaken to treat it with method, to arrange it, to classify it—in one word, to master it in its whole extent. It is yet a new subject."[3]

That observation of Jeremy Bentham's is still true. Sanctions, or the methods that exist for the realization of policies, may be thought of as constituting the armory of government. But even a catalogue of that armory is not in existence. Far worse, no knowledge exists of the fields in which its weapons have been employed. And the weapons themselves are many. The criminal penalty, the civil penalty, the resort to the injunctive side of equity, the tripling of damage claims, the informer's share, the usefulness of mere publicity as a means for coercing action, the license as a condition of pursuing certain conduct, the confiscation of offending property—these repre-

2. Bentham, *Theory of Legislation* (2d ed. 1871), p. 358.
3. *Id.,* p. 359.

sent only a few of the many weapons in that armory. Their effectiveness to control conduct in one field, their ineffectiveness to achieve that same control in another field have never been scientifically stated. Why is it, for example, that the informer's share, a method commonly employed in colonial legislation, has generally disappeared from the statute books but nevertheless still survives in the field of customs collection? What leads to the device of permitting a litigant to recover triple damages for certain injuries, and how effective is that claim to bring about enforcement of the law by this effort to stimulate individual initiative? Questions such as these, which can so readily be put, have as yet failed to stir research. Far less have they received even tentative answers.

One of the most interesting devices for the imposition of sanctions frequently characterizes the administrative process. This device blends within a single administrative agency both the power to initiate complaints and the power to determine whether the alleged facts which give rise to the complaint exist to such a degree as to justify the imposition of a penalty. Few aspects of the administrative process have been more criticized. Doubts as to the desirability of combining these functions were expressed by the Committee on Ministers' Powers which in 1932, at the request of the Lord Chancellor, surveyed the operations and the directions of the administrative process in England.[4] In 1936 the American Bar Association's Special Committee on Administrative Law

4. *Report of Committee on Ministers' Powers* (1932), pp. 76–79.

condemned that procedure in no uncertain language.[5]
The argument that leads to its condemnation usually
reads as follows: A first and fundamental principle
of natural justice is that no man shall be judge in his
own cause; a tribunal that has enforcing functions
has by that fact an interest in the outcome of the litigation to which it is a party and hence should not
take part in the process of decision. That psycho-
logical interest, as the Committee on Ministers' Powers observes, may be more compelling than even a
pecuniary interest, inasmuch as the tribunal will feel
under some pressure to defend a policy which it may
have initiated, or at least to establish the fact that its
earlier judgment to prosecute was justified.

Before examining the merits of these contentions
it is worth while to try and understand how that device arose, for it seems curious that a combination of
functions which is said to violate "the first and most
fundamental principle of natural justice" has
achieved such a foothold in the American scheme of
administrative law.

An examination of the origins of this blending of
functions indicates that in part it is a natural historical development and that in part its creation was
deliberate. A significant incidence of the use of this
device lies in the field of immigration control. The
exclusion and expulsion of aliens, either because of
illegal entry or because they have proved themselves
undesirable elements of our society, was subjected to
administrative adjudication, partly because the pres-

---

5. (1936) 61 Am.Bar Ass'n.Rep. 735. See also (1934) 59 Am.
Bar Ass'n.Rep. 545.

sure of the innumerable cases that arose was too great for the ordinary machinery of government. A more significant reason, however, was the conception that the whole field of control over the exclusion and expulsion of aliens lay within the appropriate exercise of executive power. A right, in the sense of a right enforceable in a court of law, was not deemed to inhere in an alien seeking entry to our shores, or wishing to make his home with us. It was regarded as more a privilege than a right, something that could be withheld or granted not only within the discretion of the Congress but within such a discretion as the Congress might choose to vest in executive officials. Considerations such as these led to providing for administrative adjudication in this field by the same officers who had the duty of enforcing the standards as they might be delineated by the legislative or by the executive.[6]

The most significant combination of these two functions in the federal administrative process occurred in 1914 at the time of the passage of the Federal Trade Commission Act. After a bitter political fight in which President Wilson used all the resources that he could command, the Federal Trade Commission was equipped with the power to issue cease and desist orders. The method there employed has been the model for the grant of similar powers to other administrative agencies and therefore de-

6. Cf. Chae Chan Ping v. United States, 130 U.S. 581 (1889); Nishimura Ekiu v. United States, 142 U.S. 651 (1892); Fong Yue Ting v. United States, 149 U.S. 698 (1893); Lem Moon Sing v. United States, 158 U.S. 538 (1895); Yamataya v. Fisher, 189 U.S. 86 (1903); United States v. Sing Tuck, 194 U.S. 161 (1904).

serves some analysis. The cease and desist order is issued by the Commission to prevent the pursuit of an unfair method of competition by a respondent. The proceeding is initiated by complaint which emanates from the Commission after the determination on its part, first, that there is probable cause for believing that the law has been violated, and, second, that there is a public interest in restraining the allegedly illegal conduct.[7] After the complaint is issued, a hearing upon that complaint is held before the Commission, or some subordinate official, in which counsel for the Commission try to establish the truth of the allegations that have been made by the Commission. After the hearing, the Commission makes up its mind whether or not the allegations that it originally made have been established, and if it concludes that they have, a cease and desist order is thereupon issued. It should be noted that in these cases prior to the issuance of a complaint, a very thorough examination is made of the activities of the respondent. Voluminous evidence is accumulated which is all tested and retested in order to determine whether it tends to reveal that the respondent has been engaging in the alleged practices. This is especially true with reference to such an administrative agency as the Securities and Exchange Commission, which has the right to conduct preliminary examinations under oath.[8] Here the record prior to the issuance of the complaint is even less *ex parte* in character, because of the examinations

7. For the procedure of the Federal Trade Commission see 1935 ANN. REP. F.T.C. 43.

8. Securities Act, § 19; Securities Exchange Act, § 21(a).

and cross-examinations under oath of the parties involved. The case against the respondent is quite fully
rounded out by the time that the complaint is issued.[9]
Though the finding of the Commission necessary to
the issuance of a complaint is technically merely a
finding that the Commission has reason to believe
that the defendant has engaged in these activities,
there is the danger that the mental processes that
lead to that conclusion may differ only by a matter
of emphasis from a judgment that the defendant has
engaged in these practices. The issuance of a complaint itself may be so disastrous to a respondent,
because of the seriousness of the accusation, that substantial evidence that he has engaged in the alleged
illegal practices must and should properly be forth-
coming before that preliminary step is taken.

No one can fail to recognize that there are dangers
implicit in this combination of functions in an administrative agency. The curious fact remains, however, that the tendency toward this combination has
been notably upon the increase. The reasons that
underlie the passage of a particular statute may on
occasion be dismissed as capricious or as poorly
founded. But to dismiss lightly a long continuing
and definite legislative development is, perhaps, to
miss deep-seated causes that underlie a succession of
practical legislative judgments.

Inquiry as to the nature of these causes will reveal
that they center about inadequacies attending the
judicial process in the settling of those claims that
have been committed to the administrative for pro-

9. See In the Matter of White, Weld & Co., 1 S.E.C. 574 (1936).

tection. It would, for example, have been possible in 1914 to have made the Federal Trade Commission simply another specialized arm of the Attorney General's office, for the actual remedial device given to that agency was similar to an injunction issued by a court of equity. But in the field of industrial regulation deep and enduring disappointments had already resulted from the judicial attitude toward railroad legislation and toward the Sherman Act. Judicial interpretation of the statutory standards laid down by the Congress plainly gave the judges power to mold the statute to their own conceptions; and that molding had too frequently set at naught the public and political effort which had so hopefully expended itself in the passage of the statute. Judicial interpretation suffered not only from inexpertness but more from the slowness of that process to attune itself to the demands of the day. There was thus hesitation by the Congress to wait for the viewpoint of the judiciary to tally with the growing conceptions that an administrative agency might evolve as a consequence of its continuing concern with the well-being of industry. Of this lag in the judicial process, Dicey, in his *Lectures on the Relation of Law and Public Opinion in England during the Nineteenth Century,* had occasion to make these remarks. He says, speaking of the strict construction given by the judges to the Common Law Procedure Act of 1854:

However this may be, we may, at any rate as regards the nineteenth century, lay it down as a rule that judge-made law has, owing to the training and age of our judges, tended at any given moment to represent the convictions of an earlier era than the ideas represented by parliamentary legislation. If a statute, as already stated, is apt to reproduce the public opinion not so much of today as of yesterday, judge-made law occasionally represents the opinion of the day before yesterday.[10]

To lodge a great, interpretative power in the judiciary involved the risk that a policy, which initially was given to the administrative to formulate, might be thwarted at its most significant fulcrum by judgments antagonistic to its own.

These reasons, which were responsible for placing adjudication in the hands of the administrative in the case of the Federal Trade Commission, were more patently present when the administrative had large powers of rule-making. They were also active in fields, such as labor, which revealed continuing judicial sterilization of legislative attempts to equip workmen with the ability to use their bargaining power. The Clayton Act, which was heralded as labor's Magna Charta because it was thought to be a shield against the application of the Sherman Act to labor combinations, was literally destroyed by judicial interpretation.[11] It is true that the language

10. Dicey, *Law and Opinion in England* (2d ed., 1926), p. 369.

11. Indeed, the real effect of the Clayton Act was to multiply for labor organizations the burden of the Sherman Act. Section 16 of that Act gave a new remedy against labor combinations in the right it accorded private parties to enjoin violations of the Sherman Act. "Of a total of 64 proceedings of all kinds brought against labor under the Sherman Act after the passage of the Clayton Act, 34, or more than one half, were private injunction suits. The law may thus be said to have more than doubled the chances that labor activities would be hampered by the Sherman Act. This is indeed a curious though probably a most important consequence of a law which labor greeted as its charter of industrial freedom." Berman, *Labor and the Sherman Act* (1930), p. 103.

of that Act did not compel a different judicial attitude, but no trace of the will that prompted the legislative to suggest some different treatment of labor
combinations can be found seeping through to the
decisions. Administrative adjudication thus was re-
sorted to in the field of labor in the hope that it would
buttress the legislative will to turn the existing current of judicial decision.

Intelligent coördination between policy-making
and enforcement is, of course, essential in the business of regulating industrial enterprise. If such
qualities as flexibility and expertness are demanded
in the field of rule-making, the intensity of that demand is no less in the area of adjudication. To place
adjudication outside the administrative process would
tend to threaten the carrying through of those policies whose formulation was so deliberately given to
the administrative. But the fact that there is this
fusion of prosecution and adjudication in a single
administrative agency does not imply the absence
of all checks. It implies simply the absence of the
traditional check. And so it becomes worth while to
examine those checks that actually inhere in the administrative process to safeguard it against the rise
of arbitrariness in the imposition of administrative
penalties.

An examination of the administrative process
shows the presence of several checks. The first is the
fact that that process, as distinguished from the judicial process, moves in a narrow field. Even in that
field its discretion, as we have seen, is bounded by
limitations that hem in the delegation to it of the
power to act. The human claims that come before it

for consideration are thus limited. The administrative is not open to the broad range of human sympathies to which the judicial process is subject. Again, as an agency of government confined to a fairly narrow field, its singleness of concern quickly develops a professionalism of spirit—an attitude that perhaps more than rules affords assurance of informed and balanced judgments. Precedents and habits as to the disposition of claims quickly tend to make its discretion, such as it is, the "equitable discretion" of a Court of Chancery. Thirdly, a statutory condition of its power to act by way of order is normally the requirement of findings of fact necessary to support an order—findings of fact that must be both detailed and informative. A fourth check, too often ignored, springs from the relationship of adjudication to policy. I have referred to the fact that the necessity for their conformance brought adjudication under the wing of the administrative. But the necessity for this conformance also affords a check upon adjudication. The policies initiated by the administrative must be "right" from an industrial standpoint. They must promote the economic soundness of the industry subject to the charge of the administrative. The same considerations, however, lead to "rightness" in the disposition of claims. For arbitrariness and unfairness in adjudication will as easily wreck the regulatory controls of the administrative as those same qualities on the rule-making side.

A fifth factor that operates against the intrusion of impertinent considerations into the process of adjudication is the tendency, so manifest in recent times, to divorce the administrative process from a too obvious connection with the executive by making it an independent tribunal. Recent developments have emphasized this trend. Of the ten independent agencies referred to by the President's Committee on Administrative Management, nine have been created since 1913, and five since 1933. At the same time this quality of independence is being strengthened. An examination of the constituent statutes will show that the terms of the members of independent commissions have been increased, their tenure has been strengthened, and the significance of their position has been enhanced.

An ultimate check is, of course, the right to judicial review. It is interesting to observe that despite the outcry against the combination in one administrative agency of the functions of prosecution and adjudication, the tendency over the past few decades has been to decrease rather than to increase the power of judges to impose checks upon the exercise of administrative power. Judicial review has been narrowed rather than broadened. A statutory provision that is now almost traditional enjoins judicial reversal of administrative action if any evidence exists to support the administrative finding. The administrative determination is thus given the strength of a jury verdict rather than the finding of an equity court. Typical of the increasing limitations being placed upon judicial review is the series of statutes, beginning with the Expediting Act of 1903,[12] which place limitations upon the power of a single judge

12. Act of February 11, 1903, 32 STAT. 823.

by injunction to restrain and annul administrative action.[13] In other words, the protest of the theorists against the absence of checks is contradicted by the course of practical legislative judgments which are limiting the checks that now exist.

I do not mean to imply, from this analysis of the reasons that have led to the combination in a single administrative agency of the initiation and decision of complaints, that the process is not susceptible to abuse. Reasons of great weight, however, have made for that fusion. It is in the light of these reasons which take into consideration the assets as well as the liabilities of such a combination that the desirability of continuing such an institution must be weighed. The most outstanding of these liabilities may briefly be sketched. The process of administrative adjudication has a greater susceptibility to interference from members of the executive and legislative departments than the same process has when pursued by a court. It is neither unusual, nor is it considered contrary to the rules of the game, except by a sensitive few,[14] to speak or to write a word for a party under scrutiny

13. See Frankfurter and Fisher, *The Business of the Supreme Court at the October Terms, 1935 and 1936* (1938) 51 Harv.L. Rev. 577, 603–618.

14. Illustrative of these sensitive few is the following incident that revolves about Senator George W. Norris of Nebraska. On November 17, 1936, the Senator wrote to the Chairman of the Securities and Exchange Commission:

"I am enclosing a copy of a letter which I have just written to Mr. Leo C. Tilsley regarding some case which the Bankers Union Life Company now has before your Commission in which there is some controversy about their right, under the law, to issue securities. I do not know whether you care to go into this matter or not but it occurred to me that this Company is improperly trying to

in an administrative proceeding. And due to the dependence of the administrative upon these other branches of government suggestions of this character tend to be given some weight. But the fact that restraints upon such intervention do characterize judicial proceedings springs more from habits and traditions of long standing. A similar development with reference to the administrative seems more a matter of time than of political theory, of demonstration by the administrative that intervention of this character

influence your Commission. I want you to know of the attempt that is being made to influence your Commission by this Corporation."

The accompanying letter to Mr. Tilsley follows:

"I have read with a great deal of care the letter, dated October seventeenth, 1936, from your President and the President of the Bankers Union Life Company. I have also read your letter of October seventeenth directed to me and the memorandum signed by you and left at my office yesterday afternoon.

"As I stated to you in our conversation, I have no information whatever as to the difficulty that seems to exist between the Bankers Union Life Company and the Securities and Exchange Commission at Washington. It is true that the President of your Company, in his letter of October seventeenth, has given me his viewpoint and the claims set up by one side of this controversy. It would be manifestly improper for me, even if I had the authority, to pass upon the merits of the question or to form an opinion or judgment upon hearing only one side of the controversy. In the next place, I have no authority to act. The Securities and Exchange Commission has jurisdiction and control over this controversy. Of course, I am interested in the proper enforcement of the law and I have no reason to believe that this Commission will do anything that is not right and proper under the law. For me to try to use my influence, if I have any, as a Senator in this controversy would, in my judgment, be very improper. It would be similar to writing to a judge, having a case under advisement, and trying to influence his decision.

"What you are asking me to do is to use my influence to expedite this hearing, or to ask the Commission to render a decision in

is futile and tends more to prejudice than to further a client's cause.

Some gain against the consequences of so combining functions has been achieved by providing for the separation of these functions in the administrative agency's staff. Adjudication, as distinguished from the presentation of claims, is generally centered in trial examiners who, as a matter of internal organization, are not subordinated to any official other than to the Commission itself. The adequate development

this controversy at once. When I take into consideration the facts disclosed by this correspondence, and from our conversation, that you have made this same appeal to Senators and Governors in Colorado, Wyoming, and South Dakota, and to my colleague, Senator Burke from Nebraska, I cannot help but feel as though the real object is to influence the decision by getting as much political influence as possible to bear upon the matter and to show to this Commission that, behind you, are all the prominent officials of the various States in which your corporation does business.

"It seems to me it would be manifestly improper for me to use any influence I may have to secure immediate action by the Commission. I cannot get away from the idea that the real object is to influence the Commission upon the merits of the case. I cannot see why, if you have a good case, and are fully complying with the law, you should try to get all the prominent men in these States to intercede in your behalf before this Commission.

"In the memorandum you left at my office yesterday, you called my attention to several prominent Nebraska people who were very active in my campaign at the recent election and who are now engaged in some way in your behalf in this controversy. You ask me to see them and to communicate with them. If you have a meritorious case, I do not understand how this could be of assistance to you. It seems to me that the one object of it all is to get political influence behind your application now pending before the Securities and Exchange Commission at Washington.

"I am asked by the President of the Bankers Union Life Company, in his letter, to write to Honorable James M. Landis, Chairman of the Securities and Exchange Commission, and to impress upon him the harm that will be done to over 1,000 investors and over 3,000 innocent policy holders. I do not see how I can attempt

of these staffs would provide judges who have, as they should have, an understanding of the general policy of the administrative, indeed a proper bias toward its point of view, and yet, by having been entirely disassociated with the earlier phases of the proceeding, have no personal interest in its outcome. Today trial examiners' staffs on the whole have too little competence. The reasons for this are many, but one of the most outstanding springs in many agencies from the rigid requirements of civil service rules, rules which, in defiance of the administrative's own desires, place these important individuals within

to influence the action of the Chairman of the Securities and Exchange Commission when I have no knowledge in regard to the controversy except that which is entirely ex-parte. It would be improper for me to do this even if I had made a study of the case and examined all the papers and documents on file. Why should I, because I happen to be a Senator from Nebraska, try to argue this case before the Commission? You have attorneys and I assume they have made a proper investigation of the case. Why are you interesting a dozen or more Senators, and several Governors, to whom similar appeals have been made, to argue your case? Would they not be acting as attorneys in the matter?

"I cannot resist the impression made upon me by these letters that the real attempt is to undertake to win your case before the Securities and Exchange Commission by getting the Governors and Senators of various States to act as attorneys and argue in your behalf. Of course, some of these Senators and Governors are not even attorneys. I take it that they would not have it known by the public and by their constituents that they were acting as attorneys because such action would be improper, unprofessional and unethical if not absolutely illegal.

"Under the circumstances, I must decline to take the action that you and the President of your company persistently insist I take."

The case to which this correspondence referred was disposed of by the Commission by the issuance of a stop order. See In the Matter of Bankers Union Life Company, Securities Act Release No. 1278 (1937). (The correspondence is quoted by permission of Senator Norris and of the Securities and Exchange Commission.)

a classification that entitles them to a salary of only $4,600 a year. It is impossible to expect for that price those qualities that are necessary to make a good trial examiner—experience in the disposition of business and wide knowledge of the field of regulatory activity. Because of these limitations, the Securities and Exchange Commission was led not to use its regular trial examiners for the conduct of difficult cases but to hire outside experts for that purpose, or to assign a lawyer in the General Counsel's office to a particular proceeding. Both of these devices had their virtue but, at the same time, failed to promote the building of a permanent judicial force.

A further factor that makes against administrative adjudication having those qualities that it should appropriately have is that the members of an administrative agency rarely have the time and opportunity for thoroughly scrutinizing a record and coming to their own conclusions as to what it establishes. Their other functions may be so time-consuming that the actual process of adjudication is delegated, subject to only slight supervision. The worst consequence is the practice of reaching conclusions without articulation of the reasons that underlie them. This practice, which the Supreme Court of the United States has more than once condemned when employed by inferior judges, still characterizes, in the main, the work of the Federal Trade Commission. Its adjudications take the form of a stereotyped finding of the facts followed by a purely formal conclusion upon the law. There is but little doubt in my mind that that practice was in part responsible for the unfortunate encounters that the Federal Trade

Commission for years had with the courts.[15] But even though delegation may not lead to this result, it will mean that the laborious process of articulation is not indulged in by the individual who has the responsibility of judgment. Any judge can testify to the experience of working on opinions that won't write with the result that his conclusions are changed because of his inability to state to his satisfaction the reasons upon which they depend. Delegation of opinion writing has the danger of forcing a cavalier treatment of a record in order to support a conclusion reached only upon a superficial examination of that record. General impressions rather than that tightness that derives from the articulation of reasons may thus govern the trend of administrative adjudication.

Despite disadvantages such as these, the net balance would still seem to favor leaving adjudication with the administrative. The necessity for coördinating enforcement with policy is still so urgent as not to lead lightly toward the divorcement of these functions. Furthermore, if the real concern arising from the fusion of adjudication and prosecution in one agency is that of arbitrariness in the administrative, separation of these two functions will hardly do away with the chief reason for that concern. Some fifteen years ago a survey of the administration of criminal justice in Cleveland brought dramatically to the attention of the public the fact that the chief law-enforcing officer of that community was not the crimi-

15. See the criticism of this practice in Henderson, *Federal Trade Commission* (1924), p. 334.

nal judge but the district attorney.[16] The survey established, what is true in every community, that of the many individuals who were arrested by the police only a relatively small percentage were brought to trial. The acceptance of a plea of guilty or the entry of a *nolle prosequi* disposed of the vast majority of criminal defendants. The administrative process poses the same problem.

The outlines of the Securities Act of 1933 are generally known, but they can be briefly rehearsed here. An effective registration statement is a prerequisite to the public offering of securities by means of the mails or any other instrumentalities of interstate commerce. Prior to the acquisition of such an effective registration statement, no sales or even solicitations of offers to buy can be made by the sponsors of the security issue or by any broker or dealer, except that underwriting arrangements between the issuer and the underwriter can be, indeed must be, concluded prior to the effective date. The acquisition of an effective registration statement flows from the passage of time. No approval of the administrative is required. Effectiveness results from its inaction in initiating a proceeding for a stop order within twenty days after the filing of the statement. Or, in the event that amendments to that statement have been filed, effectiveness derives from consent to their filing.

The proceeding for a stop order is brought by the Commission before the Commission. The hearing may be short or it may continue for weeks. The order it-

16. See *Criminal Justice in Cleveland* (1922), Part II.

self flows from a finding that the registration statement contains false or misleading statements of fact as to the matters that are required to be set forth in it. The order is reviewable in court, but its issuance destroys the effective quality of the statement, or, in the event that the statement has not yet become effective, prevents it from becoming effective. The selling of securities subsequently to the issuance of the stop order constitutes criminal conduct and as such is punishable in the ordinary manner.

A few outstanding characteristics of this proceeding deserve notice. The first is that despite the issuance of hundreds of stop orders, no effort has yet been made to review in court the issuance by the Commission of any such order.[17] The second is that in practically no case which concerned a security issue sponsored by leading and assumedly reputable underwriters has there as yet been even the initiation of a stop order proceeding. The reasons for these two phenomena are not, on the one hand, the legal unassailability of the Commission's work, or, on the other, the absence of misstatements of fact attending the registration statements filed in connection with issues sponsored by leading underwriters. The real reason is that the legal remedy of judicial review has in these cases no practical content. The ability to sell a substantial block of securities depends upon creation of a belief that that issue is, like Calpurnia, above suspicion. It depends further upon a wise choice as to the time for offering the securities to the

17. Since the writing of the above statement an appeal has been taken from the Commission's order in In the Matter of Oklahoma–Texas Trust, Securities Act Release No. 1563 (1937).

public. The very institution of proceedings is frequently sufficient to destroy the former quality, for the Commission's allegation that some untruthfulness attends their registration is sufficient to create grave suspicion as to their merit. The threat to institute proceedings, furthermore, will mean delay and even though the proceedings may later be dismissed by the Commission, or eventually by a court, the time that elapses before such relief can be procured will have permanently chilled the market for the securities. Administrative adjudication in these cases is, to all intents and purposes, final. But more than this, the threat of initiating a proceeding, because of its tendency to assail the reputation of an issue and because it will mean delay, is sufficient in the normal case to bring about compliance with the desires of the administrative.

The significant power that is exercised by the administrative in these cases is in its capacity as prosecutor rather than as judge. The major reforms in regard to underwriting practice, corporate disclosure, and accounting techniques that the Commission has brought about—and it has brought about many—are not of public record. The trend of decisional policy is not readily discoverable from the stop order opinions of the Commission. The nature of these reforms can only be found by an examination of the successive amendments made by issuers of securities prior to the effective date—amendments made in the hope that the corrected form of disclosure will avert the bringing of a proceeding. In a situation such as this the cure for arbitrariness with regard to administrative action does not lie in the divorcement of the prosecutory and adjudicative functions of the administrative. Checks upon arbitrariness here must lie within the administrative itself.

The same characteristics will be found to attend other aspects of the administrative action. The initiation of a complaint is public. Of itself it is an attack upon the conduct of the respondent. Situated as the administrative is at the center of news distribution in this country, the complaint receives wide publicity, frequently far wider publicity than its disposition receives. The proceeding that was instituted by the Securities Exchange Commission against Michael J. Meehan to suspend or expel him from the New York Stock Exchange, on the ground that he had been engaged in manipulative activities, was headline news not only in New York but in many other sections of the country. The opinion of the Commission finding him guilty was matter that was relegated to the financial page. The same characteristics will be found to have attended the proceedings initiated by the Federal Trade Commission against the Goodyear Tire and Rubber Company in the effort to compel them to cease giving preferential treatment to Sears, Roebuck and Company in the sale to them of Goodyear Tires under the All State trade name. I advert to this power to prosecute primarily to emphasize the point that the charge of arbitrariness, which is commonly made against administrative action, usually appertains to the exercise of the power to prosecute rather than to the power to adjudicate. It is restraints upon the exercise of that power that in my judgment are of far greater significance than the creation of restraints upon the power to adjudicate.

The nature of what those restraints can be, I have referred to before—professionalism in spirit, the recognition that arbitrariness in the enforcement of a policy will destroy its effectiveness, and freedom from intervening irrelevant considerations.

In discussing the functioning of the administrative as related to the sanctions that it employs, I have noted the rise of the independent, regulatory administrative agency. The reasons for favoring this form seem simple enough—a desire to have the fashioning of industrial policy removed to a degree from political influence. At the same time, there seems to have been a hope that the independent agency would make for more professionalism than that which characterized the normal executive department. Policies would thus be more permanent and could be fashioned with greater foresight than might attend their shaping under conditions where the dominance of executive power was pronounced. Again, the idea of the independent Commission seems naturally to have evolved from the very concept of administrative power. That power embraces functions exercisable by all three branches of government. To have taken these functions and to have placed them in the hands of any one of the three branches of government would have seemed incongruous. The natural solution was to place them beyond the immediate control of any one of the three branches, yet subject to checks by each of them.

The history of the last fifty years will show a correlation between the creation of the independent agency and broad grants of administrative power. Regulatory developments that relied for their enforcement directly upon the courts are illustrative of the partial delegation of administrative power. In instances of this nature, the impulse that leads to the creation of an independent agency is absent. Thus as long as the control of monopolistic practices was sought purely through the sanctions of normal judicial penalties there was no need for an administrative agency. Similarly in 1906 when the federal government sought to prohibit the sale of adulterated food and drugs very little was called for in the way of policy-shaping or rule-making. Administrative remedies to bring about enforcement were not created. Instead, enforcement of the Food and Drugs Act, as well as the Meat Inspection Act of 1907, was intrusted to an executive department. In these instances what was envisaged for the future related primarily to an evolution of enforcement and not an evolution by the enforcing agency of policy. This line of delineation will generally be found to differentiate the independent from the nonindependent agencies. Conspicuous exceptions, such as the delegation of administrative power to the Secretary of Agriculture under the Packers and Stockyards Act, sometimes resulted from political pressure. Here the regulated industry, the packers, used its power to transfer governmental control over its activities to an agency that was believed to be more amenable to political coercion. The packers' experience with the Federal Trade Commission, from their standpoint, had been unfortunate and they hoped to get more favorable treatment by the lodgment of control in an executive department. But viewed broadly, independence seems to be the rule of political growth for administrative power, rather than the exception.

It is difficult to appraise, even in general terms, the importance of making the administrative agency independent. In a field such as this, so much rests on surmise that there is a tendency to throw the mantle of universality about the few limited particulars that one can discover. But such evidence as there is indicates that there have been gains. Railroad policies, for example, have achieved a degree of permanence and consistency that they might not have possessed had their formulation been too closely identified with the varying tempers of changing administrations. Though the drive against monopoly on the part of the Federal Trade Commission dwindled into a mere campaign against false advertising, as the philosophy of the Coolidge and Harding administrations became dominant, at the same time that Commission pursued with intensity and, in the face of political opposition, its investigation of the utilities. The history of the Tariff Commission, despite the fact that it is little more than an investigative agency, demonstrates a want of complete subserviency to the wishes of the executive. Considerable popular opposition was aroused when President Coolidge, by his use of the power of appointment, sought to change the statutory tenure of its officers into a tenure at the pleasure of the executive.[18] The Federal Power Commission only succeeded in becoming an active agency when, in 1930, it was reconstituted and put upon an

18. See testimony of D. J. Lewis in the *New York Times,* June 2, 1926.

independent basis. On the other hand, professionalism in the nonindependent agencies has suffered on occasion at the hands of political superiors. The story of the administration of the Food and Drugs Act reveals several instances of an inexplicable reversal of policy emanating from above.[19] For years the enforcement of the Packers and Stockyards Act and the Grain Futures Act seems to have reflected a certain complacency of attitude toward the objectives of those statutes held by the succeeding Secretaries of Agriculture.

The available facts in the field are few—perhaps too fragmentary upon which to theorize. One must, however, recognize that the personality of a chief can dominate the atmosphere as well as the outlook of an entire force of subordinates. Men, in government and out, are too prone to accept leadership wherever and whenever they find it. Powers of the head of a department are penetrating and pervasive. By a judicious selection of personnel, discrimination in promotions, a shifting of responsibilities, his views can only too easily control the staff. Interposing the head of a department between the active administrative official and the public means insulating the administrative official from the public and consequently depriving him of a sounding-board for his views. The chief of a bureau possesses no public position comparable to that of the head of an independent administrative agency. Support for his policy must derive from, or through, his chief and not directly from the public. To that degree he lacks the ability to withstand at-

19. See Hayes and Ruff, *The Administration of the Federal Food & Drugs Act* (1933) 1 L. & CONTEMPORARY PROBLEMS 16, 22.

tack or to gather support for his views. And since the quality of his professional approach to his regulatory problems must filter through his superior, public appraisal of his performance is likely to rest upon a partial, incomplete, and perhaps unknown record.

The concept of the independent Commission recently received additional support when, in 1935, the Supreme Court of the United States, in the so-called "Humphreys Case,"[20] surprised the legal profession by cavalierly throwing aside its earlier considered observations in the case of *Meyers* v. *United States*,[21] and held that the Congress could place a member of an independent Commission beyond the reach of an unlimited executive power of removal. The decision is more important for the judicial recognition which it gives the independent agency than for the actual protection that it accords its members. For unless the issue between the executive and a member of an independent Commission is of great moment, it is hardly to be expected that a member of one of these Commissions would continue to hold his position in the face of an executive policy that is powerful enough to have its views realized despite the opposition of that member. The real significance of the Humphrey doctrine lies rather in its endorsement of administrative freedom of movement. It underwrites the legislative desire for protection of the administrative from interference as to the disposition of de-

20. Rathbun v. United States, 295 U.S. 602 (1935).
21. 272 U.S. 52 (1926). See Frankfurter and Hart, *The Business of the Supreme Court at the October Term, 1934* (1935) 49 HARV. L.REV. 68, 105.

tail, which in so great a measure is the objective sought by the creation of the independent Commission.

If the political desires underlying the creation of independent commissions extend not merely to assuring freedom from interference in the process of adjudication but also to an assurance of nonintervention with reference to the initiation of complaints and the formulation of a program of action, this form of governmental mechanism is likely to endure. The difficulties that attend it result from the danger of its pursuing a policy that runs counter to the general direction of the executive. The danger, however, is more apparent than real. Executive policy to be effective needs the support of the legislature and when these two forces combine, their effect is such that the administrative cannot pursue a course of action contradictory to their desires. The real danger to the executive from the independent Commission lies in the possibility of inaction on the part of its members. Inertness may flow from the quality of the personnel of a Commission, but more frequently it flows from the lack of centralization of responsibility in the Commission itself. The practice adopted by the Interstate Commerce Commission of annually rotating its chairman, a practice followed by the Federal Trade Commission, means that the chairman is little more than the presiding officer at the meetings of the Commission. No particular responsibility attaches to that position and consequently no policy emanates from it. The real liaison officer between the Commission and the executive or the legislative may be another member and the formulation of policy may lie in his hands. In the absence of a permanent chairman, the internal organization of the agency tends to arrange itself so as to have no directing officer, so that though the agency is a repository of executive power, it actually has no executive. A change to the practice of a permanent chairman would do much to focus public responsibility and to bring about the possibility of more effective coördination between the various agencies and the executive.

A discussion of the administrative process as a means for the imposition of sanctions seems to me a necessary prelude to the discussion of the sanctions themselves. But that prelude makes it impossible to consider now at length the various sanctions that the administrative process is today employing. I can only call attention to two tendencies in the employment of sanctions that I think are of great significance. The first is the increasing use of the licensing power. Its employment in the federal administrative field is of very recent origin. Prior to the World War federal legislation will show but slight resort to this method. Administratively imposed restraints were direct. Even in 1914, when the Federal Trade Commission Act was passed, the only method there employed to bring about compliance with administrative policy was a type of administrative injunction. The beginnings of the use of the licensing power are to be found in utilities and radio legislation, where the idea of a license naturally springs from the conception of a permit to use property over which the federal government has some control. In the Transportation Act of 1920 and the Securities Act of 1933 the license or permit attaches itself rather to the privilege of doing an act than to the privilege of continuing in a business. In the Grain Futures Act and in the Securities Exchange Act of 1934 the licensing device is employed with reference to an institution as a whole. Commodity markets and securities exchanges were required to be registered as a condition of continuing in business. The Securities Exchange Act extended that theory to the members of the exchanges, giving the administrative power to expel or suspend members of exchanges whose conduct failed to conform with the prescribed standards. By regulation the power was extended to cover the entire field of brokers and dealers, so that their right to continue in business depends upon conformance with required standards. The Motor Carriers Act of 1935 in its requirement for brokerage licenses and permits for contract carriers shows an interesting resort to the same device. The suggestions for federal incorporation made in such legislation as the Borah-O'Mahoney bill again rest upon an extension of the concept.[22] The strength of such a device is, of course, obvious, for the right to pursue a given livelihood, so important in these days of specialization, is dependent in its entirety upon the observation of prescribed standards of conduct.

A second tendency is to be found in those fields where government possesses the power to grant privileges of great economic content. It tends to withhold or revoke those privileges dependent upon compli-

22. The licensing device was also widely employed under the National Industrial Recovery Act and the Agricultural Adjustment Administration Act.

ance with standards deemed essential for the well-being of a particular industry. Government as a source of credit, as a source of supply, as consumer, possesses powers which frequently are broader in their implications than those that it has in its capacity simply to inflict punishment. Agencies often classified as nonregulatory, such as the Federal Reserve Board, the Federal Deposit Insurance Corporation, the Reconstruction Finance Corporation, and the United States Maritime Commission, derive their strength to control the economic direction of various industries by the utilization of these devices. The government as purchaser was far more effective in bringing about conformance with the codes of fair competition under the National Industrial Recovery Act than was the government as policeman. The discovery of the effectiveness of that sanction led, of course, to the Walsh-Healey Act, when the direct effort to control conditions of labor seemed to have met insurmountable constitutional obstacles.

This search for effective regulatory sanctions continues. It is the weakness of the sanctions yet devised that threatens rather than their effectiveness. Moreover, it is the weakness of the administrative method as a mechanism of control that should be our generation's worry, not its effectiveness. It is due to this weakness that we are led to the use of taxation as a method of encouraging obedience to standards of doing business. The pursuit of other means is not proscribed but heavy costs are thereby entailed. Immense power, of course, resides in the employment of taxation avowedly for social ends. Normally, however, it suffers from an inability to provide flexibility of treatment and continuity of concern with given segments of our industrial civilization—attributes that characterize the administrative process. Further, because of the wide standardization that taxation requires, its use may have implications which are not easily foreseen and which result in unanticipated shifts in industrial activity. Adjustments thus have constantly to be made and these adjustments are likely to be bent by the pressure for revenue. But, even more, they are likely to suffer from the fact that the responsibility for the solution of the general problem is in hands too close to the political scene, too occupied to acquire that understanding of the facts essential to form judgment, too harried by the intellectually consuming demands of the subject matter. Taxation in the domestic field when employed to effectuate policies or to favor one interest as against another is likely to pass through all the vicissitudes that have, since Hamilton's day, attended the tariff. Of these, perhaps the chief is that expertness is viewed with resentment and informed advice given but scanty recognition.

One other tendency arising out of the absence of effective sanctions is the employment by government of the forces of economic competition. The initiative behind the movement of placing government directly in business derives in part from the belief that certain enterprises possess such great public significance that their pursuit and control cannot be intrusted to private industry. The charges for the services that they render are paid by so many members of the community that they are, as Mr. Justice Brandeis observed with reference to railroad rates, "in the nature of a tax."[23] Convictions of this character lead government to the direct assumption of responsibility for the conduct of the mails, the maintenance of our roads, supplying communities with water, light, and power. But this extension of governmental activity has received an enormous impetus from our failure to provide effective administrative sanctions. Particularly true is this of the utility field. Despair over the ability of the administrative adequately to provide for reasonable rates has led to the effort of government to effect that reduction by offering an equivalent service on a cheaper basis. In the utility field, as well as in the railroad field, the nonexistence of adequate sanctions to protect people against corrupt financial practices, the consequences of which are to be seen in the costs that thereby have been fastened upon the enterprise, is leading to a demand for government control. In the field of banking, the same tendencies are active. It is not without moment that the economic effectiveness of the resort by government to this device today disturbs private enterprise far more than the employment of administrative methods of regulation. Or, to put it concretely, the private utilities fear the Holding Company Act less than they do the Tennessee Valley Authority.

Some years ago, before I had the occasion to participate actively in government, I made a plea in the name of science for a study of sanctions.[24] Today I would reiterate that plea not merely because of a

23. New England Divisions Case, 261 U.S. 184 (1923).
24. See Landis, *The Study of Legislation in Law Schools* (1931) 39 HARV.GRAD.MAG. 433.

scientific concern with the problem, but because of a deep political concern. The demand for the assumption by government of the responsibility to direct and control enterprise increases day by day in intensity. But study of the practical limits of administrative action is still too dormant. The instruments of power that we believe we have created too frequently tend to become mere pulpits from which to hurl thunderbolts of talk, not control rooms where the touch of a button releases power or enjoins its surge.

To essay what we cannot do is often worse than to do nothing, for failure destroys too easily the dream of better ways of living. So much in the way of hope for the regulation of enterprise, for the realization of claims to a better livelihood has, since the turn of the century, been made to rest upon the administrative process. To arm it with the means to effectuate those hopes is but to preserve the current of American living. To leave it powerless to achieve its purposes is to imperil too greatly the things that we have learned to hold dear.

IV. ADMINISTRATIVE POLICIES
AND THE COURTS

THE most fascinating branch of American constitutional law relates to judicial review over legislative action. Here one is presented with decisions that speak of contest between two agencies of government—one, like St. George, eternally refreshing its vigor from the stream of democratic desires, the other majestically girding itself with the wisdom of the ages. Similarly, in the field of administrative law judicial review over administrative action gives a sense of battle. Courts are not unconscious of the fact that, due to their own inadequacies, areas of government formerly within their control have been handed over to administrative agencies for supervision. The legislative judgments underlying such a partitioning of government do not always convince. Thus, under the guise of constitutional and statutory interpretation, efforts to thwart the effects of those legislative judgments are not uncommon.

An approach to the problem of judicial review cannot neglect the fact that its essence springs from the Anglo-American conception of the "supremacy of law" or "rule of law," as it is variously called. Dicey in 1885 had occasion to define its essence as follows: "We mean," he says, speaking of the rule of law, "in the first place, that no man is punishable or can be lawfully made to suffer in body or goods except for a distinct breach of law established in the

ordinary legal manner before the ordinary Courts of
the land. . . ."[1]

That definition practically excludes the idea of
administrative adjudication except to the extent that
the administrative can report its conclusions to a
court. It implies the right to a trial *de novo* before a
judicial tribunal. However truly that may have described the area of the administrative process in
1885, it is a misdescription of the scope of the rule of
law as it exists today.

In 1936 Mr. Justice Brandeis essayed a more modern definition. "The supremacy of law," he states,
"demands that there shall be opportunity to have
some court decide whether an erroneous rule of law
was applied; and whether the proceeding in which
facts were adjudicated was conducted regularly."[2]
Two elements, according to this, flow from the concept of the "supremacy of law"—the right of a party
to a judicial determination as to the appropriate
rule of law applicable to his particular case, and the
right to a judicial determination as to the regularity
of the procedure employed by the administrative.
Mr. Justice Brandeis' analysis of the place of the
"supremacy of law" was, however, made in protest
against the insistence on the part of the majority of
the Court of a right to review findings of fact made
by an administrative agency.

The area in which the courts insist that administrative findings of fact cannot be final is an interesting one. It seems odd, very odd, as a three-judge

1. Dicey, *Law of the Constitution* (8th ed. 1923), p. 183.
2. St. Joseph Stock Yards Co. v. United States, 298 U.S. 38, 84
(1936).

court has expressed it, that a Constitution "which expressly makes findings of fact by a jury of inexperienced laymen, if supported by substantial evidence, conclusive . . . prohibits Congress making findings of fact by a highly trained and especially qualified administrative agency likewise conclusive, provided they are supported by substantial evidence."[3]

Prior to the rise of regulatory administrative agencies, the determination of whether a particular rate charged by a common carrier was a reasonable one could be had in an ordinary judicial tribunal. The function of adjudicating upon the reasonableness of that rate was naturally, as an analytic matter, the exercise of judicial power, because it was a thing that courts did. The inadequacies of that process to deal with the rate problems of a national system of railroads led to the institution of administrative agencies. But prior to the rise of the administrative method of handling these issues, the Granger legislatures of the Middle Western states decided to deal directly with the problem of unreasonable and discriminatory rates. By statute maximum rates were established for certain roads, and in 1877 the validity of that method of handling the rate problem was upheld by the Supreme Court.[4] Little was then known, however, of the proper basis of rate-making. The judicial process had developed no appropriate

3. St. Joseph Stock Yards Co. v. United States, 11 F. Supp. 322, 327 (W. D. Mo. 1935).
4. Munn v. Illinois, 94 U.S. 113 (1877); Chicago, B. & Q. R.R. v. Iowa, 94 U.S. 155 (1877); Peck v. Chicago & N. W. Ry., 94 U.S. 164 (1877); Chicago, M. & St. P. R.R. v. Ackley, 94 U.S. 179 (1877); Winona & St. P. R.R. v. Blake, 94 U.S. 180 (1877).

theories because its prior dealing with the problem had been merely through litigation involving individual rates, and the judgments setting aside particular rates did not force the courts to consider the effect of this process of supervising rates upon the operating revenues of the carrier as a whole. As rate-making developed upon a large scale, it became clear that rate schedules could make or break a carrier as well as make or break a community or an industry. Some floor had to be created below which rates could not be compelled to drop, and the courts set themselves to find that floor. Meanwhile, the technical difficulties of legislative rate-making became so apparent that the legislatures created administrative agencies and delegated the task to them.

Rate-making thus, by the turn of the century, appeared to be more of a legislative power than a judicial power. The administrative was seen as taking the place of the legislature so that its functioning was easier to analogize to the exercise of power by the legislative branch of government than by the judicial branch. The fact that the administrative acted with reference to the rate situation as a whole rather than limiting its consideration to the reasonableness of a rate as between a particular shipper and a carrier, and the fact that its orders were commands for the future and not merely judgments as to the justifiability of a past exaction, led the courts to classify its power in this respect as a legislative power.[5] At the same time constitutional prohibitions against the strict legislative exercise of the rate-making power

5. Prentis v. Atlantic Coast Line Co., 211 U.S. 210, 226 (1908).

were in the process of development. Rates, the Court said, could not be so low as to be confiscatory.[6] Later "confiscatory" was elaborated to be the establishment of rates so low as not to yield a reasonable return upon the value of the property devoted to the business.[7] But "value," in turn, had to be elaborated. Standards, which we need not examine for the moment, were set up to point to the factors upon which judgments as to "value" should rest, standards whose application left open wide areas for differences of opinion as to the weight to be attached to the various facts that related to value.

The argument for insisting upon the necessity for an independent judicial determination of findings of fact establishing values can be neatly stated in the form of a syllogism.[8] Rate-making is an appropriate exercise of the legislative power provided that the rates are not confiscatory. Whether or not they are confiscatory depends upon the correctness of the finding as to value. The facts relating to value must thus be independently found by a court in order for a court to conclude that a particular legislative act was within the legislative power; otherwise the legislature would itself be finding the facts upon which

6. Reagan v. Farmers' Loan & Trust Co., 154 U.S. 362 (1894). For earlier expressions, see Stone v. Farmers' Loan & Trust Co., 116 U.S. 307, 331 (1886); Dow v. Beidelman, 125 U.S. 680, 689 (1888); Georgia R.R. & Banking Co. v. Smith, 128 U.S. 174, 179 (1888); Chicago, M. & St. P. Ry. Co. v. Minnesota, 134 U.S. 418, 455 (1890); Chicago & G. T. Ry. v. Wellman, 143 U.S. 339, 344 (1892).

7. Smyth v. Ames, 169 U.S. 466 (1898).

8. See Buchanan, *The Ohio Valley Water Company Case and the Valuation of Railroads* (1927) 40 HARV.L.REV. 1033, 1037; Comment (1936) 50 HARV.L.REV. 78, 83.

the very exercise of legislative power depends. It was thus not enough for a court to satisfy itself that the trier of the facts, the administrative, had followed the correct rules as to valuation. Instead, the actual determination of value had to be made by the court.

It was this reasoning that led the Supreme Court of the United States in 1920, in the *Ohio Valley Water* case,[9] to hold unconstitutional a Pennsylvania statute which the Pennsylvania courts had concluded limited the right of judicial review over administrative determination of value, to inquiry simply as to whether there was evidence to support the administrative finding. More was required by the Constitution in order for the Court to be sure that the purported exercise of legislative power was really an exercise of such power, and this was an independent judicial determination upon the facts relating to value. Similarly, in 1936, the Court in the *St. Joseph Stock Yards* case,[10] though it upheld an order of the Secretary of Agriculture fixing the maximum rates that could be charged by a stockyards company, insisted that the Constitution required a court not merely to find that the Secretary had evidence upon which to reach his findings as to the value of the property, but to find of its own accord that upon the same evidence the Court would reach the same conclusion as to the value of the property.[11]

9. Ohio Valley Water Co. v. Ben Avon Borough, 253 U.S. 287 (1920).

10. See note 2, *supra*.

11. The distinction between mere review over administrative determination and insistence upon independent judicial determination of the facts has been aptly summarized by the court in St. Joseph Stock Yards Co. v. United States, 11 F. Supp. 322, 327

This does not mean that in every proceeding in which valuation is in issue an administrative finding does not have the same finality as a jury verdict. Law refuses to be that simple. In tax cases or in condemnation cases when the amount due from, or payable to, a party depends upon the valuation of property, an administrative finding on valuation is final if supported by evidence. No independent judicial determination of value is required.[12] True, the same type of syllogistic reasoning might be advanced in cases of this character. For the constitutionality of the exaction of any particular sum depends upon whether the appropriate ratio exists between the charge and the valuation of the property. Error in valuation would mean an unconstitutional exaction, so that to prevent an unconstitutional exercise of power an independent judicial determination as to value should be had. Proceedings in tax and condemnation cases, however, are so like ordinary judicial

(1935), as follows: "When it is said that an independent judgment must be reached by the court, it is meant that the court's findings must be determined by the weight of the evidence and not by a consideration as to whether the findings of the administrative agency are supported by substantial evidence or are arbitrary. A finding may well be supported by substantial evidence and still be against the weight of the evidence. The advocates of each of the two theories, (1) that the Court must give its independent judgment on the record made and that, (2) it must accord a de novo hearing, agree that the findings of the administrative agency should be looked upon as presumptively correct. That is far less, however, than an acceptance of the findings of the administrative agency as conclusive if they are supported by substantial evidence or are not arbitrary."

12. Bauman v. Ross, 167 U.S. 548 (1897); Long Island Water Supply Co. v. Brooklyn, 166 U.S. 685 (1897); Crane v. Hahlo, 258 U.S. 142 (1922); San Diego Land & Town Co. v. Jasper, 189 U.S. 439 (1903); Kentucky R.R. Tax Cases, 115 U.S. 321 (1885).

proceedings that the readier analogy for the Court in these cases is to liken administrative adjudication to judicial adjudication. In the latter, findings of fact by juries are conclusive if supported by evidence; so by analogy findings of administrative tribunals in tax cases were given the same degree of finality.

A similar problem arose shortly after the enactment of the Longshoremen's and Harbor Workers' Compensation Act.[13] The story of the effort to extend the benefits of workmen's compensation to persons engaged in maritime employment is a grim comedy of errors. After two futile attempts to bring these persons within the operation of state workmen's compensation legislation,[14] the Congress in 1927 set up a system, modeled upon the state workmen's compensation laws, to govern workers within the admiralty jurisdiction of the United States. The constitutional power of the Congress in this respect extends only to the admiralty jurisdiction. Whether or not a particular employee at a particular time is within that jurisdiction involves not only hyper-technical questions of law but depends also upon what the facts with reference to his employment and the situs of the injury are found to be.[15] Furthermore, his right to compensation rests, among other things, upon his ability to establish the existence of an employer-

13. Act of March 4, 1927, c. 509, 44 STAT. 1424.

14. Southern Pacific Co. v. Jensen, 244 U.S. 205 (1917); Knickerbocker Ice Co. v. Stewart, 253 U.S. 149 (1920); Washington v. Dawson & Co., 264 U.S. 219 (1924). See Palfrey, *The Common Law Courts and the Law of the Sea* (1923) 36 HARV.L.REV. 777; Comment (1924) 37 HARV.L.REV. 478.

15. Comment (1927) 40 HARV.L.REV. 485.

employee relationship at the time of the injury. In
1932 in *Crowell* v. *Benson*[16] the Court held that administrative findings of fact on these two issues could
not be made final, in the sense that they should stand
if there was substantial evidence to support them.
Instead, these two facts being jurisdictional in the
sense that the constitutional power of the Congress
could extend only to certain states of fact, an independent judicial determination had to be had with
reference to them. The syllogism here is again apparent. Constitutional power, according to the Court,
extended only to the admiralty jurisdiction and only
to the imposition of absolute liability where the em-
ployer-employee relationship existed. Constitutional
power to deal with the relationships involved in any
particular case, therefore, depended upon the existence of certain facts, and unless those facts were
found by a court no assurance could be had that the
particular case lay within the sphere of the federal
admiralty jurisdiction. The argument of the minority
that such syllogistic reasoning had equal application
to other facts upon which the issue of liability depended, was ignored by the majority, as well as the
plea that a sensible administration of justice demanded that a degree of finality should attach to administrative findings of fact.

I shall give a further illustration of the incidence
of this doctrine relating to so-called jurisdictional or
constitutional facts as it concerns another field. The
power of the administrative to exclude or deport an
alien depends upon whether a particular individual
is in fact an alien. Indeed, the constitutional limits

16. 285 U.S. 22 (1932).

of the power to exclude or deport depend upon that issue of alienage. An administrative finding of fact that an individual is not a citizen but an alien is final when the issue is one of exclusion.[17] But when the issue is one of deportation, such finality ceases to attach to that administrative finding. Instead, the party threatened with deportation is entitled to an independent judicial determination of his claim that he is a citizen of the United States.[18]

On the basis of logic the series of cases relating to jurisdictional and constitutional facts is irreconcilable with those that grant finality to administrative determinations of fact. They seem equally indefensible from the standpoint of practical judgments as to the appropriate area of administrative activity. It is true that in the deportation and exclusion cases two great differences of a practical nature are to be found. The first is that the process of exclusion, because of the number of aliens seeking entry, demands something akin to a summary procedure, whereas deportation exerts no such pressure either in numbers or in the necessity for speed of disposition.[19] The second is that the penalty of deportation normally has more serious consequences. It tears up and disrupts the pursuit of a livelihood that has already been entered upon; exclusion simply denies the right to find new surroundings for living.

But if we move from these cases to the others, practical judgments as to the desirability of court

17. United States v. Ju Toy, 198 U.S. 253 (1905).
18. Ng Fung Ho v. White, 259 U.S. 276 (1922).
19. See Van Vleck, *The Administrative Control of Aliens* (1932), p. 210.

intervention fail to tally with the legalistic conclusions. In the field of rate-making the effect of the *Ohio Valley Water* case, coupled with the insistence of the Court that reproduction cost must be given fair consideration in the determination of value, has been to prolong interminably the process of administrative rate-making. A delay of ten or fifteen years, an expenditure of millions of dollars, constant interruption of administrative proceedings by appeals to the courts, have brought the regulatory process into contempt. The practice of appealing to the Court on every issue of fact relating to valuation has transformed what should be a businesslike proceeding into a bitter, wrangling lawyers' battle. That after these many years of the effort to develop workable regulatory controls, the New York State Commission on the Revision of the Public Service Commissions Law can report that "effective regulation along the lines originally intended by the Act has broken down,"[20] spells little in the way of credit to the judicial molding of the area of administrative rate regulation.

In the field of workmen's compensation judicial review of administrative findings of jurisdictional fact has equally little to commend it. If *Crowell* v. *Benson* is to require the reintroduction into the administration of workmen's compensation legislation of the necessity for independent judicial determination of those facts upon which the jurisdiction of the administrative rests—to say nothing of its intimation that a trial *de novo* upon these issues is required—the very efficiency of the system becomes threatened.

20. *New York State Commission on Revision of the Public Service Commissions Law, Report of Commissioners* (1930), p. 1.

Judicial review upon the issue of interstate commerce, as that issue is raised by litigation under the Federal Employers' Liability Act, had little to commend it. After twenty-five years of incessant litigation the boundaries of that Act were still undefined. Yet, in those twenty-five years, it was before the Supreme Court 172 times.[21] A judgment upon such a problem as is involved in questions such as that Act raised, or upon issues of fact such as those presented by *Crowell* v. *Benson,* as distinguished from a judgment establishing a rule of conduct, has neither force as a precedent nor as a decision is it capable of analogical development. It settles that case alone, and opening up such determinations to appellate review makes against the finality that should attach to litigation, particularly in these fields. One especially unfortunate effect attaching to judicial intervention in cases of this character has been aptly summarized by Mr. Justice Brandeis in his comment on the practical effect of *Crowell* v. *Benson* on the administration of the Longshoremen's and Harbor Workers' Compensation Act. "Since," he says, "the advantage of prolonged litigation lies with the party able to bear heavy expenses, the purpose of the Act will in part be defeated."[22]

The insistence that the administrative process in these phases must be subject to judicial review is to be explained in part, I believe, by economic determinism. But the deeper answer lies in our traditional notions of "law" as being rules administered and de-

---

21. Schoene and Watson, *Workmen's Compensation on Interstate Railways* (1934) 47 HARV.L.REV. 389.

22. Crowell v. Benson, 285 U.S. 22, 94 (1932).

veloped by courts. We must remember that until a comparatively short time ago Anglo-American government was essentially government by judges. The great mass of our law was developed by the resolution of conflicting claims in courts where the governing rules were evolved by the judge. In contract, in tort, in negotiable instruments, in trusts—the body of our law is judge-made and represents the successive reactions to practical situations of a professional class that was nurtured in the same traditions and was subject to the limitations of the same discipline.[23] That class has had pride in its handiwork. Nor can one deny its right to pride. But the claim to pride tends, especially in the hands of lesser men, to be a boast of perfection. It is a rare greatness that recognizes experience as the life of the law. A lesser vision, fearful of the frailty of human thought and human judgment, claims Delphic powers, and rests the learning of the law upon an affinity with deep and mysterious principles of justice that none but itself can grasp. Deep resentment thus attaches to any criticism of its inadequacies, any suggestion as to its biases. To admit to the dispensation of justice other individuals, no matter how wise, who are not bound by the older disciplines, is regarded with horror.

Chief Justice Hughes, in addressing the Federal Bar Association in 1931, speaks of the growth of administrative law in the following fashion:

A host of controversies as to provisional rights are no longer decided in courts. Administrative authority, within a con-

23. Landis, *Business Policy and the Courts* (1937) 27 YALE REV. 235.

stantly widening sphere of action, and subject only to the limitations of certain broad principles, establishes particular rules, finds the facts, and decides as to particular rights. The power of administrative bodies to make findings of fact which may be treated as conclusive, if there is evidence both ways, is a power of enormous consequence. An unscrupulous administrator might be tempted to say, "Let me find the facts for the people of my country, and I care little who lays down the general principles." We all recognize that this development has been to a great extent a necessary one . . . Experience, expertness and continuity of supervision, which could only be had by administrative agencies in a particular field, have come to be imperatively needed. But these new methods put us to new tests, and the serious question of the future is whether we have enough of the old spirit which gave us our institutions to save them from being overwhelmed.[24]

But it is just because some of those old institutions had proved inept for a modern society that a new spirit has sought to shift their emphasis.

I spoke before of the issue of judicial review over administrative action giving one the sense of battle. Nowhere does that more clearly come to the surface than in the recent case of *Jones* v. *Securities and Exchange Commission.*[25] In the early days of the administration of the Securities Act of 1933 the question was raised of how to handle a registrant's request to be permitted to withdraw his registration statement prior to its effectiveness. Examination of a registration statement filed with the Commission might give rise to a belief that some of the assertions

24. *New York Times,* February 13, 1931, p. 18.
25. 298 U.S. 1 (1936).

it contained were false. A quiet investigation into the facts would then be made, and, if this gave ground for that belief, stop order proceedings would then be initiated. To avoid public exposure of an attempt to defraud the public, a registrant might seek to withdraw. The withdrawal of the statement would, it is true, operate to prevent the acquisition of any right to offer to the public the securities that were sought to be registered. As such it had an effect similar to the entry of a stop order. But misstatement of material facts and the avowed attempt to defraud the public seemed to the Commission serious matters. To allow a registrant to escape the consequences that should flow from such misconduct by the simple act of withdrawing his registration statement appeared inadequate. It was possible, as a theoretical matter, to try to indict a registrant whose misstatements had been deliberate; but the chances of conviction for crime, when, due to the vigilance of the administrative, no one had been defrauded, are doubtful.[26] The better course seemed to be to establish a record of fraud after a hearing and in such a manner inform the investment world of the fraud that was attempted and the character of parties to it. With that in mind, a rule was adopted making withdrawal depend upon the consent of the Commission, and a practice was pursued of denying withdrawals whenever there was reasonable ground to believe that deliberate, material misstatements had been made by a registrant.

26. Two parties involved in the stock promotion, the facts of which are set forth in In the Matter of Continental Distillers and Importers Corporation [1 S.E.C. 54 (1935)], were indicted in the Supreme Court of the District of Columbia but were acquitted.

In 1936 the validity of that practice was challenged in the Supreme Court of the United States. Doubt quite generally existed as to the power of the Commission to promulgate a rule governing withdrawals in view of the silence of the statute upon the subject of withdrawals; but assuming the validity of the rule, the exercise of discretion to deny withdrawals in the manner indicated seemed quite appropriate. The Supreme Court, however, took a different view. It assumed that the general rule was valid but denied any power to the Commission to refuse withdrawals in cases where the registration statement was still ineffective and where no securities had as yet been sold.

Such a result was not too surprising. But the process of thought by which the Court reached its conclusion still startles. By analogical reasoning of a familiar character, the Court likened the stop order proceeding to a suit in equity. Then finding that the equity practice permitted a plaintiff to withdraw his suit at any time, if that withdrawal would not prejudice the defendant, it concluded that this equity practice must bind the Commission. Consequently the Commission should not have denied the request of the particular registrant to withdraw his statement. Had the Court stopped there, one might have regretted its conclusion as weighting the scales in favor of fraudulent promoters, but that would have been all. Had the case involved a misapplication of the equity practice by any inferior judge, the Court would have stopped there, pointed out the error, and reversed his conclusion. But for the Commission not to realize that its stop order proceedings were like suits in equity and not to be aware of the equity practice was not merely to commit an error; in the words of Mr. Justice Sutherland, it was "the assumption of arbitrary power by an administrative body."[27] "The action of the Commission," Mr. Justice Sutherland thundered, "finds no support in right principle or in law. It is wholly unreasonable and arbitrary. It violates the cardinal precept upon which the constitutional safeguards of personal liberty ultimately rest—that this shall be a government of laws—because to the precise extent that the mere will of an official or an official body is permitted to take the place of allowable official discretion or to supplant the standing law as a rule of human conduct, the government ceases to be one of laws and becomes an autocracy."[28] There was more in this vein—suggestions of unreasonable search and seizure, and intimation that the Commission's action was "among those intolerable abuses of the Star Chamber, which brought that institution to an end at the hands of the Long Parliament in 1640"[29] —a remark that brought forth from Mr. Justice Cardozo the terse comment: "Historians may find hyperbole in the sanguinary simile."[30]

Such an outburst indicates that one is in a field where calm judicial temper has fled. Deep feelings underlie this unguarded language of Mr. Justice Sutherland. They underlie, too, the suggestion by the Chief Justice that the administrative is prone to abuse the powers intrusted it. Rhetoric of this nature

27. Jones v. Securities and Exchange Commission, 298 U.S. 1, 19 (1936).
28. *Id.*, 23–24.   29. *Id.*, 28.
30. *Id.*, 33.

has a purpose. If it is fair to apply the legal rule that one intends the natural and probable consequences of his acts, certainly the effect if not the purpose was to breed distrust of the administrative. Invective, such as Mr. Justice Sutherland hurled at the Commission for an action that three justices commended as "wisely conceived and lawfully adopted to foil the plans of knaves intent upon obscuring or suppressing the knowledge of their knavery"[31]—an action which, at its worst, was a pardonable technical error—was naturally seized upon by every opponent of security regulation, for none of them, even in the heat of the legislative struggle, had indulged in such hyperbole. Its effect was not to promote that calmness of atmosphere in which wise administration flourishes. For months thereafter every effort to deal with fraudulent promoters was met by the accusation that Star Chamber tactics were being employed. But worse, to the uninitiated who have neither time nor the ability to grasp the precise issue involved by a particular case, the cause of good administration suffered by this excoriation, naturally headlined by the press, of administrative action as arbitrary and violative of ancient rights and privileges.

The most disputed field of judicial review over administrative action today concerns the finality of administrative findings upon so-called issues of constitutional or jurisdictional fact. Apart from the incidence of that problem in the immigration field, the cases, upholding the claim to an independent judicial determination of these issues, have all been decided

31. *Ibid.*

by a divided Court. In the *Ohio Valley Water* case,
three justices dissented; in *Crowell* v. *Benson*, three
justices dissented; in the *St. Joseph Stock Yards*
case, three justices dissented from the conclusion of
the Court on this point, and a fourth justice, Mr.
Justice Roberts, indicated by his memorandum of
concurrence and his earlier dissent in *Crowell* v. *Benson*, doubt as to the validity of the Court's position;
in *Baltimore & Ohio R.R.* v. *United States*,[32] a case
in which the majority took occasion by way of dictum
to reiterate its views, four justices took occasion to
emphasize that they would not support the majority
on that issue. In view of these divisions, the law as to
what finality shall attach to administrative findings
of fact is likely to reflect the minority's rather than
the majority's view. Because their reasoning seems
more to accord with the temper of the times, it is
they, rather than the majority, who are likely to gain
adherents to their position.

The basis of the minority's position is thus of absorbing interest. Its rejection of the syllogistic position of the majority is unimportant. What matters
are the positive reasons advanced for its conclusions.
They group themselves about the thesis that the more
appropriate tribunal for the determination of these
issues is the administrative. Great emphasis, however, is placed upon the constitution of the adjudicating administrative agency. Its composition and its
procedure condition its fitness as an instrument for
the determination of these issues. Mr. Justice Brandeis twice notes that in these cases the Court is not

32. 298 U.S. 349 (1936).

dealing with informal, summary administrative action based on *ex parte* casual inspection or unverified information, where "no record is preserved of the evidence on which the official acted," but "with formal, deliberate quasi-judicial decisions of administrative tribunals, based on findings of fact expressed in writing, and made after hearing evidence and argument under the sanctions and the safeguards attending judicial proceedings."[33] The choice by the legislature of such a procedure for the determination of these issues of fact is thus not deemed by him to involve a violation of the due process clause.

The minority is not only sympathetic with the administrative process; it hopes to encourage its capacity to dispose more effectively of the business intrusted to it. It fears that the majority doctrine, by reserving judgment on these issues to the courts, will imperil the responsibility that should attend the administrative process. Indeed, a world of difference in temper and in outlook separates the denunciatory fervor of Mr. Justice Sutherland in the *Jones* case from the hope of the administrative process that inheres in Mr. Justice Brandeis' observation—"Responsibility is the great developer of men."[34]

The positive reason for declining judicial review over administrative findings of fact is the belief that the expertness of the administrative, if guarded by adequate procedures, can be trusted to determine these issues as capably as judges. If so, it is only delay that results from insistence upon independent

33. St. Joseph Stock Yards Co. v. United States, 298 U.S. 38, 81 (1936); see also Crowell v. Benson, 285 U.S. 22, 88 (1932).

34. St. Joseph Stock Yards Co. v. United States, 298 U.S. 38, 92 (1936).

judicial examination of the administrative's conclusion. This evaluation of the scope of judicial considerations in terms of administrative expertness points to the reasons for the differentiation of treatment between the rate-making cases and the immigration cases. The minority has explained that distinction upon two bases. One is that the adjudications are not made by quasi-judicial administrative agencies that transact their business in a manner similar to courts. This premise, however, is questionable in view of the internal organization of the office of the Commissioner of Immigration. The other basis is that the right involved is more than a property right; it is the right to the liberty of the person. It is true that the claim *"Civis romanus sum"* echoes down the ages with more power to stir the heart than a claim that property has been undervalued. One cannot criticize a magistrate who feels an urge to give it every protection that he can. But apart from these bases for distinction, it should be observed that the issue of citizenship is triable in a simple manner. Little in the way of expertness is demanded for its determination. The record of facts that underlies its establishment is a simple one. In their most extended form such records do not reach the 3,466 pages that the Court had before it in the *St. Joseph Stock Yards* case. That, after all, was "rate regulation in its simplest form," as contrasted with the 36,893 pages, not including 3,324 exhibits, that comprised the record before the District Court in the *New York Telephone Company* rate case.[35]

If the extent of judicial review is being shaped, as

35. *Id.,* 90.

I believe, by reference to an appreciation of the qualities of expertness for decision that the administrative may possess, important consequences follow. The constitution of the administrative and the procedure employed by it become of great importance. That these factors already in part mold the scope of judicial review is apparent from the decisions. Different agencies receive different treatment from the courts. A reputation for fairness and thoroughness that attaches to a particular agency seeps through to the judges and affects them in their treatment of its decisions. Fairness and thoroughness may also be apparent upon the record as it reaches the court, so as to lead the court to the conclusion that the evidence has received the attention that it deserved and that it would have received in the hands of one trained in legal techniques.

The interesting problem as to the future of judicial review over administrative action is the extent to which judges will withdraw, not from reviewing findings of fact, but conclusions upon law. If the withdrawal is due to the belief that these issues of fact are best handled by experts, a similar impulse to withdraw should become manifest in the field of law. This problem can be seen better, I think, if put concretely. An administrative finding in a rate-making controversy as to the value of a particular generating station, made after hearing and upon evidence, we may assume will hereafter be final. The administrative, whose daily concern is the consideration of these matters, is recognized to possess greater competence in appreciating the bearing and weight of testimony upon that issue than would characterize either a judge or a jury. For this reason to allow finality to rest with the administrative violates no constitutional prohibition. But the same considerations of expertness have validity in the field of law. A determination by an administrative agency that a particular trade practice is an unfair method of competition is a determination theoretically not of fact but of law. But despite the assumed expertness of the administrative in weighing the economic consequences attendant upon that practice, its decision as yet has no finality. The scope of judicial review in such a case is wholly different.

I use these terms "fact" and "law" knowing how tenuous the distinction between them is. Professor Dickinson in his study on *Administrative Justice and the Supremacy of Law in the United States* rejects the distinction completely. He says:

In truth the distinction between "questions of law" and "questions of fact" really gives little help in determining how far the courts will review; and for the good reason that there is no fixed distinction. They are not two mutually exclusive *kinds* of questions, based upon a difference of subject-matter. Matters of law grow downward into roots of fact, and matters of fact reach upward, without a break, into matters of law. . . . It would seem that when the courts are unwilling to review, they are tempted to explain by the easy device of calling the question one of "fact," and when otherwise disposed, they say that it is a question of "law."[36]

It is impossible to disagree with this statement as a description of the present state of the decisions

36. Dickinson, *Administrative Justice and the Supremacy of Law in the United States* (1927), p. 55.

dealing with judicial review of administrative action. But the rejection of the distinction, though it may accord with the fact, leaves nothing upon which to base a philosophy as to the appropriate spheres of administrative and judicial activity. If our basic constitutional conceptions adhere to a belief in the "supremacy of law"—a belief in an inviolable area for the resolution of claims by courts—it must give some content to the word "law." Collecting the cases and illustrating how the scope of judicial review varies with reference to different administrative agencies and different areas of activity will give a picture of its operation. But such an analysis fails to satisfy the demands for a creative philosophy that seeks a basis upon which to allot law-making by adjudication as between courts and administrative.

Section 10(a) of the Securities Exchange Act authorized the Commission in connection with the purchase or sale of any securities to proscribe by rule or regulation, as the Commission might deem necessary or appropriate in the public interest or for the protection of investors, the use of "any manipulative or deceptive device or contrivance." By the amendments of 1936 brokers and dealers in the over-the-counter market were forbidden to effect transactions in securities by means of "any manipulative, deceptive, or other fraudulent device or contrivance," and the Commission was empowered by rule or regulation to "define such devices or contrivances as are manipulative, deceptive or otherwise fraudulent." Pursuant to the authority granted by these sections the Commission adopted a series of rules forbidding certain specified practices that it conceived to be "manipulative, deceptive or fraudulent." Among them is the requirement that a broker or dealer who controls, or is controlled by, the issuer of a security must disclose the existence of that control before entering into any contract with a customer for the purchase or sale of that security. Another rule forbids a broker or dealer who handles a discretionary account to make purchases or sales in that account which are excessive in size or frequency, in view of the financial resources and character of that account. A third forbids a distributing broker or dealer to offer securities "at the market" unless he believes that a market exists for that security other than such as he or his associates may create.

Here are samples of law-making by regulation, specifically pricking out the content of the statutory concept of "manipulative, deceptive and fraudulent" devices. The authority of the Commission to promulgate and enforce these rules can, of course, be tested in court. Such a suit would raise the issue of whether the action taken was within the authority granted to the Commission. That issue would lead the court generally to consider whether the particular conduct described in any particular rule could fairly be called "manipulative, deceptive or fraudulent." But the court would hardly ask itself whether it would, of its own accord, have prescribed such a rule. In other words, the scope of judicial review in such a case would be somewhat akin to that of judicial review over the validity of legislation challenged under the due process clause. A reasonable belief held by the administrative, since it was acting in the manner of a legislature, that such practices tended to promote fraud and deceit in the security markets would, in all probability, be sufficient upon which to base the validity of the rule. The administrative judgment upon this issue would tend further to have much weight because of its assumed expertness.

It is true that in three recent cases the Supreme Court of the United States indulged in talk to the effect that the promulgation of such regulations in order to have validity must be buttressed by findings of fact.[37] How far this suggestion should be taken seriously is a matter of considerable doubt. Rules of this character are themselves evidence of administrative judgment that the particular conduct embraced by them does normally promote fraud and deceit. A further recital to that effect would be a matter of mere formality. The evidence upon which the conclusions that lead to the adoption of such rules rests is rarely of a type that is legally admissible for the patent reason that it was not gathered for the purpose of introducing it in an adversary proceeding. It resembles more the type of evidence adduced in a hearing before a Congressional committee. In the main it consists of opinions of men acquainted with

37. Panama Refining Co. v. Ryan, 293 U.S. 388 (1935); United States v. Baltimore & Ohio R.R. Co., 293 U.S. 454 (1935); Schechter Poultry Corp. v. United States, 295 U.S. 495 (1935). The force of these cases is, perhaps, diminished by the decision in Pacific States Box & Basket Co. v. White, 296 U.S. 176 (1935). See Feller, *Prospectus for the Further Study of Federal Administrative Law* (1938) 47 YALE L.J. 647, 668. The Supreme Court there sought to distinguish between regulations that were "general legislation" and "an administrative order in the nature of a judgment directed against an individual concern," saying that the former for their validity needed no findings of fact. See Landis, *The Study of Legislation in Law Schools* (1931) 39 HARV.GRAD.MAG. 433, 441.

the practices of the security markets. Instances may have come to the attention of the administrative of actual losses caused by those practices which thus focused the Commission's attention upon the desirability of putting an end to conduct of that type. But the ultimate judgment of the administrative rests on considerations that evolved out of a wide range of experience and observation and out of its study of security practices. To set them forth in detail would make a treatise on practices in the over-the-counter market rather than a limited series of recitals. To require this range of evidence to be reduced to findings of fact is as equally unrealistic as to impose a requirement upon legislatures that specific findings of fact must be a prelude to the passage of legislation.[38] These suggestions of the Court that findings of fact are a condition precedent to administrative rule-making have yet to be elaborated before their meaning can be understood.

The incidence of judicial review over administrative law-making by way of rules can be contrasted with the scope of judicial review in cases where the law-making of the administrative flows from adjudication. Under Section 5 of the Federal Trade Commission Act the administrative is authorized to restrain "unfair methods of competition" in interstate commerce. No express power to define unfair competition by regulation was granted to the Commission. Instead, the pricking out of such rules as alone

38. But see Oppenheimer, *The Supreme Court and Administrative Law* (1937) 37 Col. L. Rev. 1, 15. I have had occasion elsewhere to comment upon the desirability of recitals, but to lift them to the level of jurisdictional requirements seems unrealistic.

can make real the nature of "unfair methods of competition" was to come from the process of adjudication. Judicial review over these decisions takes on a different character. The Court now avowedly inquires into the wisdom of any particular rule that the administrative may have evolved and considers its likeness to existing doctrine in the field. In the first case under this Section to reach the Supreme Court, *Federal Trade Commission* v. *Gratz*,[39] the Commission had ruled that the refusal of a jobber, who held a dominant and controlling position in the sale of cotton ties, to sell ties unless the purchaser would agree to buy a proportionate share of cotton bagging was an unfair method of competition. The Supreme Court reversed the Commission over the dissent of two justices. In considering the question of whether to uphold the action of the administrative the Court did not limit itself to the consideration of whether reasonable grounds existed for the Commission's conclusion. Such grounds clearly did exist. The Court instead conceived its function to embrace the right to determine independently what the appropriate rule of law should be. Its approach was identical with that which it would possess were it reviewing a legal ruling by a lower court. This remains the general doctrine. It is true that deference will be paid to the administrative judgment on the ground that it possesses some expertness with reference to the subject matter, but such deference is a matter of attitude in a particular case rather than of doctrine.

The conception that judicial review of administrative adjudication and of administrative legislation

39. 253 U.S. 421 (1920).

should be assimilated to each other has yet to gain recognition. But the problem seems essentially to have the same core. For the issues raised by the effort to find the appropriate governing rule through adjudication require appreciation and evaluation of a wide variety of business facts. In that process there is room for differences of opinion, differences that spring from the degree of emphasis placed upon these facts. The expert judgment of the administrative here, however, counts for little, for since the rule evolves as a result of the process of adjudication it now partakes of the nature of a question of law, and upon that issue an ultimate and independent judgment is said to rest with the court.

It would have added much to our ideas of the appropriate spheres for judicial and administrative activity, if the administrative in a field such as this had been given the power to evolve the meaning of "unfair methods of competition" by regulation as well as by decision. The relationship of judicial review to forms of administrative activity dealing with the same subject matter might thus have been more sharply brought into focus. As it appears now, we seem to have one of those curious paradoxes of the law. In *Truax* v. *Corrigan*[40] the Supreme Court held that the State of Arizona by legislation could not bring about a rule of law which even then, it was contended, had been established by judicial decision in the State of New York as the governing rule of human conduct.[41] In the field of administrative ac-

40. 257 U.S. 312 (1921).

41. This is the contention advanced by Mr. Justice Brandeis in his dissenting opinion. He points to the fact that in his judgment

tivity it may be that results can be reached by the process of administrative legislation which cannot be achieved through administrative adjudication.

I return thus to the issue of "law" as being the dividing line of judicial review—as bounding the province of that "supremacy of law" that is still our boast. Its content, insofar as it relates to judicial review of administrative action, reaches back to the issue of expertness. *Our desire to have courts determine questions of law is related to a belief in their possession of expertness with regard to such questions. It is from that very desire that the nature of questions of law emerges. For, in the last analysis, they seem to me to be those questions that lawyers are equipped to decide.*

To view "law" in this fashion seems to me to bring reason into our conceptions of the supremacy of law. It seems to afford some guide to molding the process of judicial review over both legislative and administrative action. It explains the variances in the scope

the Arizona statute, held unconstitutional by the majority, set forth the substance of the common law as it had been declared by the courts of Ohio, Minnesota, Montana, New York, Oklahoma, and New Hampshire. I should question, however, whether the common law of any of these states legalized the particular type of picketing involved in the Truax case, which the Supreme Court of Arizona, because of the statute, held was not subject to the injunctive processes of the state courts. Similar paradoxes are to be found. Compare, for example, the restrictions upon state legislative action in violation of the due process clause and the scope of such restrictions as applied to state judicial action. Comment (1923) 36 Harv.L.Rev. 1022; Comment (1923) 37 Harv.L.Rev. 247. See also the effort to extend the impairment of the obligation of contracts clause to protect against judicial as well as legislative action in Muhlker v. New York & Harlem R.R., 197 U.S. 544 (1905).

of judicial review over administrative agencies of different compositions and charged with the disposition of different subject matters. It lends emphasis to the insistence of Mr. Justice Brandeis that differences in treatment should be accorded to findings of fact by different administrative officials, because of differences in the facts and in the qualities of the administrative to be expert in finding the facts. It removes nothing from the insistence that policy plays a commanding role in the shaping of judicial review, but in the place of a simple theory of economic determinism, or of a barren logic, it substitutes a sense of emphasis upon intellectual quality and discipline as related to a particular problem. The line of demarcation will then speak in terms of reality, in terms of an appreciation of the limitations and abilities of men, rather than in terms of political dogma or of righteous abstractions.

Of course, such a conception of law as related to spheres of judicial and administrative activity affords no definite answers. It must not do so, for the capacities of men and the nature of disciplines will vary. But it does point to the elements that should control judgment. And from the standpoint of affording conceptions of liberty real meaning, one can ask little more than to have issues decided by those best equipped for the task.

Such a conception of the nature of law does not remove the sense of battle which dominates the question of judicial review over administrative action. But it makes that contest rest upon a plane where the issues relate to the ability of men to handle subject matter. As such, the contest should partake more of that rivalry that attends the academic scene, where a passionate desire for truth makes for recognition and not resentment of achievement.

The world of today as distinguished from that of even a hundred years ago is one of many professions. We can no longer divide it, in its civil aspect, between the church, the law, and medicine. Economics, political science, sociology, social ethics, labor economics, engineering in its various branches, all are producers of disciplines relating to the arrangement of human affairs. Government today no longer dares to rely for its administration upon the casual office-seeker. Into its service it now seeks to bring men of professional attainment in various fields and to make that service such that they will envisage governance as a career. The desires of these men to share in the mediation of human claims cannot be denied; their contributions dare not casually be tossed aside.

The grandeur that is law loses nothing from such a prospect. Instead, under its banner as a commanding discipline are enlisted armies of men dedicated to the idea of justice. But to use those armies, a sense of the effectiveness of their units is essential and an instillation in those units of morale. "Courts," as Mr. Justice Stone has reminded us, "are not the only agency of government that must be assumed to have capacity to govern";[42] nor are they, one can add, the only agency moved by the desire for justice. The power of judicial review under our traditions of government lies with the courts because of a deep belief that the heritage they hold makes them experts in

42. United States v. Butler, 297 U.S. 1, 87 (1936).

the synthesis of design. Such difficulties as have arisen have come because courts cast aside that role to assume to themselves expertness in matters of industrial health, utility engineering, railroad management, even bread baking. The rise of the administrative process represented the hope that policies to shape such fields could most adequately be developed by men bred to the facts. That hope is still dominant, but its possession bears no threat to our ideal of the "supremacy of law." Instead, it lifts it to new heights where the great judge, like a conductor of a many-tongued symphony, from what would otherwise be discord, makes known through the voice of many instruments the vision that has been given him of man's destiny upon this earth.

INDEX

THE YALE PAPERBOUNDS

27